PUBLIC ACCLAIM FOR
LAURENCE J. PINO'S INNOV
PROGRAMS AND SEMINARS

"Larry Pino is articulate, humorous, knowledgeable and quite a motivator."

—Mr. James P. Kelly,
Pittsburgh, PA

"Useful tools for anyone striving to better his or her life."

—Dave Del Dotto,
author of *Making Nothing But Money*

"Larry Pino's commitment to excellence has earned him a reputation for superiority in the money strategy game."

—Mr. Walter Feaster, Arlington, VA

"His clear-cut and concise presentations are practical illustrations of how to accumulate wealth . . ."

—David C. Eckhardt, GRI, CRS, CRB;
President, Realty Mart, Ltd.;
Past President, Tidewater Board of Realtors

"I learned more from Larry Pino in eight hours than in all fifty-six seminars I've attended in the past six years! Larry is a dynamic person with something to say!"

—Mrs. Gloria Vigil, Brookfield, WI

FINDING
YOUR
NICHE

Laurence J. Pino, Esq.

BERKLEY BOOKS, NEW YORK

FINDING YOUR NICHE

A Berkley Book / published by arrangement with
the author

PRINTING HISTORY
Berkley trade paperback edition / June 1994

ISBN: 0-425-14148-9

BERKLEY®
Berkley Books are published by The Berkley Publishing Group,
200 Madison Avenue, New York, New York 10016.
BERKLEY and the "B" design
are trademarks belonging to Berkley Publishing Corporation.

PRINTED IN THE UNITED STATES OF AMERICA

10 9 8 7 6 5 4 3 2 1

For my parents, Sam and Maria Pino,
whose constant support and
unconditional love have given me the
strength to always reach for the
best life offers and, in the process,
enabled me to find my own niche.

Contents

Acknowledgments

A BOOK OF THIS nature doesn't just simply happen; it comes from years of studying and learning and practicing, of listening and advising, of making and repairing mistakes.

To list all the people who have made a direct contribution to the development of my work would be a formidable task. I would, however, like to take the time to acknowledge those who have played a special role along the way.

First, I extend my thanks to the countless numbers of people who attended the seminars I have taught over the years. Those people were a constant inspiration and an incredible catalyst for the clarification of the fundamental messages set out in this book.

In addition, as a practicing attorney in the business and commercial fields, I owe a special debt of gratitude to the scores of clients who have allowed me, with a microscope, to see what worked and did not work for them. Out of that examination emerged a pattern that would eventually be translated into the laboratories of my seminars and the contents of this book.

Over and above each of those people, I would also like to acknowledge very specially Robert Fritz, whose book *The Path of Least Resistance* has become a classic for anyone interested in learning to be effective in every facet of life, including entrepreneurial activities; Chuck Givens, who not only allowed me to observe a marketing master in motion, but also gave me the opportunity for four solid years of weekends to interface with his seminar registrants as they attempted to do better in their lives; Mark Haroldsen, Robert Allen, Dave Del Dotto, and Mark Stoddard of the now-defunct Jefferson Institute, each of whom in a special way allowed me to observe not only what works, but in many instances what does not work, in the business field.

It goes without saying that this book would not exist today had it not been for the very patient and creative effort of Jacquelyn Denalli in continuing to work with me to make sure that what I had to say was crystal clear not only to someone who had a background in business, but to anyone first starting out. Special thanks also go to the staff of my law firm and of The Open University, with my personal acknowledgment to Lori Meade Caldwell, who never stopped prodding me to put into print what I was saying with speech, and Cathy Simmons, my long-suffering personal secretary.

Laurence J. Pino

FINDING YOUR NICHE

Introduction

SO MANY PEOPLE seem to have a curious perception of entrepreneurs as driven workaholics who have neither the time nor the interest for anything outside of their businesses. They're sometimes viewed as cocky risk takers whose personal relationships are superficial at best. They're people you might enjoy reading about in the tabloids, but you really—not really, deep down inside—don't want to be like them.

So if you don't want to be like what you think entrepreneurs have to be like, you may have decided that you're doomed to a life in the workaday world, trudging back and forth to a job, maybe a career. Your paycheck may not be quite as secure as it used to be, the economic situation being what it is, but at least it's the same amount every week. You can count on it. Can't you?

And when you are tantalized by thoughts of starting your own business, they're beaten back by the negative rhetoric about entrepreneurs. Your own personal support group—your spouse or significant other, your friends and family—may well turn into your worst enemies, as they tell you all the reasons why you can't make it in a business of your own.

They'll tell you entrepreneurs are driven people who eat, breathe, and sleep their businesses; you're not one of those. You're a well-rounded person with a variety of interests.

They'll tell you four out of five new business ventures fail within the first two years; why would you want to do something so risky?

Let me strongly advise you to ignore anyone who has a ready-made list of the disadvantages and drawbacks of entrepreneurship. This book will show you that it doesn't take a special breed of person to be an entrepreneur—just about anyone can learn to start and run a successful business. And though it's true that four out of five businesses will fail within the first two years, simply by following the techniques I'll share with you, yours can be the one out of five that succeeds.

As I travel the country talking about business, I meet thousands of actual and would-be entrepreneurs. Their backgrounds are incredibly diverse. They come from a variety of ethnic and socioeconomic groups. They have families and friends, hobbies and pets, houses and yards. They're concerned about the economy and inflation, drugs and the environment. For the most part, they comfortably fit into that category we call "normal."

What makes them different is a recognition that there's something more out there for them. They may not be sure exactly what or where it is, but they know it's there, and they want to find a way to make it work for them.

They have a desire to do something that will allow them to share in the American Dream and, in the process, more fully develop and fulfill their own lives.

And what is the American Dream? A chicken in every pot every Sunday? Home ownership? Certainly that's part of it, but it goes much deeper than political rhetoric or a few superficial possessions. It's a dream of unlimited opportunity while *we do something that is both personally and professionally satisfying.* It's a dream of emotional and material rewards. It's a dream of achievements limited only by ourselves and our imaginations.

The problem is that even though so many of us understand there's something more, we're not really sure how to get it. We don't know what's right for us, and, if by chance we figure that out, we don't know how to make it really work.

Why would you want to start your own business when the chances of failure are so high? You're not a fool, you're not crazy, and you don't have money to throw away. You don't have a lot of capital, and we all know—at least so goes the theory—that under-capitalization is the primary reason businesses fail.

But that's only the perception. The reality is that it's not lack of capital that causes businesses to fail, it's lack of understanding. Because once you understand what is right for you, and how to make that work in the proper market niche, you can create a business with a fairly accurate recognition of how much capital is required.

When under-capitalization takes the rap for a business failure, it's usually a smoke screen to cover the mistakes of an entrepreneur who chose a business wrong for himself or wrong for the market. No amount of capital, no amount of management skill, no amount of economic savvy can make up for that.

Companies that were started on a proverbial shoestring by entrepreneurs in their first business venture have thrived and made their owners wealthy because they were *right*—right for the entrepreneur and right for the market. The key to success, the kind of success that will satisfy you both emotionally and materially, is to decide on a business you are suited for, and then develop or identify a market for that business.

Who would have thought that personal computers would be almost as common in the home today as televisions were twenty-five years ago? Or that a woman offering moral support and nutritional information to others who were trying to lose weight could turn her small group into a multimillion-dollar international business? Or that an idea for a small-package overnight express service developed as a college project could become a worldwide leader in the air cargo industry? Today, Apple Computers, Weight Watchers, and Federal Express are household names—perfect examples of entrepreneurs who found their niches.

Perhaps your dreams are not on so grand a scale. You may well be searching for a business you can operate yourself, or with your spouse and just a few associates. Your ideal business may be one you can run from a spare room in your home, one that allows you to satisfy yourself while you upgrade your standard of living.

It doesn't matter whether you want to start small and stay small— but profitable—or whether you want to start small and grow large. The principles of successful entrepreneurship don't change.

And there is no mystique about entrepreneurism. Entrepreneurs are not a particular type of person. They don't come out of the same mold. They're not all clones of Donald Trump or Ted Turner—or even Larry Pino, for that matter.

Yet this mystique, this idea that entrepreneurs are a breed unto themselves, is perpetuated by current writings. The Entrepreneurial Quotient, a test devised by the Northwestern Mutual Life Insurance Company, suggests that if you didn't like group activities in school and are easily bored, you'll make a good entrepreneur. On the other hand, according to the test analysis, if the opinions of others matter to you and you don't like taking risks, you're not entrepreneurial material.

Not only is this absurd, but it may serve to deter some people from starting their own business because it reinforces their erroneous belief that they aren't suited for it.

The idea that you can or can't be an entrepreneur because of your background is, to use an old-fashioned term, complete hogwash.

Where do tests like the Entrepreneurial Quotient err? In many places. For example, group activities in school develop your leadership skills and give you an excellent foundation for dealing with others in a business situation—necessary traits for the successful entrepreneur. Boredom is more likely to occur when you're doing something you don't really want to be doing. I am an entrepreneur, but I enjoy people and I care about what they think of me. And the tens of thousands of people who have heard me speak in person and on radio or television know I don't advocate taking needless business risks, because it simply isn't necessary to operate that way.

The truth is just about anyone can be an entrepreneur. What you've done up until now doesn't matter. How much formal education you have, what types of jobs you've held, whether you've actually started a business or are just thinking about it—none of that makes any difference. What matters is that you take that first step toward realizing your dreams. Once you're on your way, you'll realize that there's no mystery, just a series of fundamental principles you can apply that will result in a successful company.

I was nineteen when I, along with my father and brother-in-law, started a sporting goods business, and since then I have been involved in an ownership capacity with forty-five companies. The sporting goods operation grew into a nine-store franchised chain before I sold it. I kept one division of the company, Braxton Recreation Company, which remains the largest institutional athletic distributor in the state of Florida. The other companies I've been involved with include a number of high-tech businesses, a copy shop, a travel agency, real estate investment companies, seven different restaurants, a publishing company, and several educational institutions.

I've also been a practicing commercial attorney for over fifteen years, providing legal representation to a variety of businesses. Since 1983, I've been lecturing on different aspects of business and money-making, talking with more people in more businesses across the country than

I could hope to count. You'll meet a lot of those people in the pages of this book.

I have learned through the real-life experience of trial and error what it takes to start and run a successful business. This book is the natural evolution of my own entrepreneurial career.

At the same time, *Finding Your Niche* is revolutionary in its simplicity. On these pages, you'll find all the tools you need to develop a failure-proof operation. The information here can be used for any type of business in any location, and is based on the simple but essential premise that understanding who you are and what you have to offer is the foundation of your success as an entrepreneur. The techniques are fundamental, easy to understand, and can be applied to either a new business venture or an existing operation.

The first concept you'll learn is integrational processing, which allows you to blend who you are with the business you would like to create and the market you'll be committing yourself to. Don't confuse this powerful process with personal development thinking. I don't teach pop psychology, and integrational processing isn't designed to compete with the abundance of self-help programs on the market. It's a unique and dynamic method of personal, professional, and market analysis that has become clear to me after years of experience and observation in the business world.

Integrational processing will allow you to develop a personal identification, a business identification, and a market identification. In your examination of these three levels, you'll use the same basic structure— a set of work sheets with questions designed to provoke answers that will provide you with the information you need. From there, you will be able to clarify your own personal commitment, create a business mission statement, and establish a market position for your company.

Next you'll learn about the primary components of a business and how they interact with one another. We'll talk about how your business can best function for positive cash management and profits. And you'll learn the six critical elements of profitability—things you can do to make any business profitable.

Because the integrational processing exercises are designed to stimulate thought, and may take some time to complete, I suggest you read the entire book through and then go back and complete the work sheets. Take your time and consider each question carefully. The answers will help you establish a foundation on which you will build the rest of your life.

You have the opportunity to create your own definition of success, and then to choose whether you want to meet that definition. Your decision should be based not only on the passion of desire, but on the confidence that comes from understanding yourself and the world in which you live.

I invite you now to make your choice.

CHAPTER ONE

Personal Identification
Who Are You Really?

"To love what you do and feel that it matters—how could anything be more fun?"
—Katherine Graham, Chairman of the Board, *Washington Post*

WHAT TYPE OF BUSINESS should you get involved with?

If you've been following the trends, you know what's hot right now. You know what the experts are touting as the up-and-coming industries of the decade. The sure things. The ones that can't miss.

Is one of them right for you?

Maybe. But maybe not.

There's more to a successful business than an economic climate ripe for a particular product or service. While that's naturally an important consideration, it's more important that your business blend with who you are: your interests, background, experience, and plans for the future.

From an academic viewpoint, there are certain fundamental principles that apply to any business and that will allow you to operate a company profitably, and we'll discuss them later on. Once you understand these principles, you will know how to make money doing just about anything. But just because you know how to make a profit selling buggy whips, does that mean you should start selling them? It depends. Certainly there's a market out there for buggy whips. Lots of cities have horse-drawn carriage tours of their downtown and historical districts, and harness racing continues to be a popular sport. The horses have to be motivated to move along by something, but if it's going to be buggy whips, do you truly care about the relative merits of different handle styles or the pros and cons of synthetic versus real leather?

Yes, people will buy buggy whips, and you could make a profit from selling them. But the question boils down to this: would you be happy doing that? And if selling buggy whips isn't the answer for you, what is?

There are thousands of business opportunities out there, and any one of them might be right for you. You could make your choice by sifting through them all, spending a considerable amount of time and money examining each one to determine which is best for you. But wouldn't it be more efficient to look inside yourself for the answer?

By using an internal method as opposed to an external one, by considering your background, experience, and desires, you can quickly eliminate the majority of those businesses because they are simply not right for you.

When you look at a business from the outside, the best you can get is a vague notion of how appropriate it is for who you are. But when you look first within yourself, you'll find not only a business idea that is right, but also where it will match the marketplace. Then you can turn it into a successful company by applying sound operational principles.

It doesn't matter whether or not your choice of business is on the experts' list of sure winners. When you are absolutely committed to an endeavor on a personal level, regardless of the potential for profit, your chances for success increase dramatically.

If that sounds simple, it is—but it is not simplistic. There is nothing inherently complicated about having your own business. In fact, when you apply the principles of integrational processing, you'll find entrepreneurship easier—and making money more satisfying—than you ever thought possible.

What Is Integrational Processing?

Integrational processing is one of the most dynamic life tools you will ever acquire. At the same time, it is so basic that its primary requirement is honest soul-searching. There are three major components, and they work—as the name implies—when they are integrated.

The whole idea of integrational processing is built on basic human needs. It revolves around an in-depth understanding of who you are and what you really want to do with your life. A natural evolution leads from that personal understanding to the knowledge of a business that is most appropriate for you and the recognition of a market you will serve.

So integrational processing deals with the development of your personal identification, your business identification, and your market identification. Once you have gone through the process, you will be able to ignore the small business failure statistics—they don't apply to you, anyway—and create a business that is virtually failure-proofed.

The structure for all three components is the same: it involves an understanding and comparison of the way things are right now and the way you want them to be. Where you are right now is your current reality; what your objectives are is your vision for the future. We'll be talking a lot about current reality and vision, because it is only when you have a clear picture of both that you'll be able to accomplish a natural forward motion. You will then have the power to create the life you want.

Now, while I have stressed that integrational processing is simple, it is not necessarily easy—ease being a very subjective term. In the few hours it takes you to read this book, I will walk you through the steps of integrational processing and show you how to use it to build a successful business. The rest is up to you. How long the actual exercises will take will depend on who you are, what you want, and how motivated you tend to be. As you develop your personal and business identification, you may find such intense self-examination psychologically difficult. The effort required by your market identification will be largely based on the results of the business segment of the process.

But no matter how much effort it requires or how long it might take, let me assure you that integrational processing does work. It worked for me, and it is working for thousands of entrepreneurs across the country who have discovered the true meaning of the American Dream. It will work for you.

Your search for the ideal business begins with the first step of integrational processing: your personal identification.

Your Current Reality

This isn't a personal achievement exercise, and though you'll set some goals, this isn't about goal setting. This is an analysis of your current reality and your vision, and it is essential if you are to move from the first to the second.

A lot of people have trouble with reality. It began when as children we were shushed by an adult for saying something that was quite true, such as "That man smells bad," or "Look, that lady is so fat she takes up two seats on the bus." The message we received was that we should pretend not to notice very obvious things.

In addition, lying about reality became a defense mechanism against authority figures who were often many times our size and weight. Did we break that vase or make that mark on the wall? It's a rare child who will admit a transgression when he or she knows punishment will follow, and that's a practice we carry with us throughout our lives.

Another problem with reality is the very human tendency to avoid pain and discomfort. Sometimes when we strip away all the excuses, reality hurts. But if integrational processing is to work for you, you must be brutally honest with yourself as you complete the work sheets at the end of the first three chapters.

Begin painting the portrait of your current reality with a clear understanding of your background, strengths, and weaknesses. If you're going to start a business, you want that business to be built on your strengths. At the same time, you need to understand your weaknesses so you can stay away from them.

Keep in mind that we are not dealing with a specific business at this point, we're dealing with who you are, and an understanding of your current reality is essential to the development of your business. Realizing who you are at this moment gives you a springboard to the future.

Though the focus of this effort is entrepreneurship, don't be limited by the list of characteristics we have come to accept as business strengths and weaknesses. That catalog includes sappy statements like "I am very detail-oriented" or "I don't have much patience with incompetent people." Go beyond the comments you might be inclined to make on a résumé or in a job interview, because the personal identification portion of integrational processing is more important to you than anything you've done before.

Forget, too, about dressing up these characteristics to make them sound pretty. No one will see them but you, so be totally candid. You're not being coached for a job interview where you need to make even the negatives sound positive. This is a private exercise. Make it worth the time and effort you're going to invest in it.

Remember, your background is rich with a combination of heredity and experience that has created personal characteristics you may not be consciously aware of. Yet these are traits that make you special, that give you the ability to perform certain functions in a uniquely effective manner—and they may not be related to how you currently make your living.

Take the case of a former law partner of mine who has only average skills as a commercial attorney. She can do the job of a lawyer, but where she really excels is as a mediator. She is tremendously empathic and instinctively knows how people operate. This gives her the ability to resolve disputes that to anyone else would seem destined for years of legal wrangling. When we worked together, I would be battling in the courtroom, and she would be settling the case in a back room. Many times, before a trial reached its midpoint, she had successfully mediated the case to the satisfaction of all parties. That she is a lawyer is frequently a minor consideration in how she operates and how she wins cases.

You, too, have traits which are absolutely independent of the job you do. You have attributes you didn't learn in school. So don't be limited by your present job description. You need to look at the entire scope of your life experiences.

My Uncle Dom was a classic example. He got into the restaurant business in South Philadelphia right after World War II. In 1983, he sold his business and took a promissory note that would generate enough income for him to live comfortably for the rest of his life. But after a year of retirement, Uncle Dom decided he wanted to go back to work. The problem was he wasn't sure what he wanted to do. I had just formulated the concept of integrational processing and was trying it out on myself and anyone else who was available. So Uncle Dom and I went out to have a few drinks and talk for a while.

That "while" was nearly five hours, during which we consumed more Scotch than I ever have since. What was significant about our discussion was that it began with Uncle Dom saying that all he really knew anything about was operating a restaurant. It ended with him realizing his horizons were much broader—because Uncle Dom did more than just run a popular restaurant.

He had a catering operation, too, which had given him the opportunity to build a tremendous network of contacts. Everybody who was anybody in South Philly had their special events catered by Uncle Dom. He was part of their weddings and anniversaries, their christenings and funerals. He knew them all. And without even thinking about what he was doing, he would routinely over the years match up someone who had a problem with someone who could provide the solution—just because he was a wonderful man and loved people.

Uncle Dom converted those contacts into a full-fledged business. From then until the day he died, he earned more as a consultant than he ever had as a restaurateur. That business came not out of his understanding of restaurants, but out of the total experience he had acquired and the contacts he had made while operating his restaurant.

So when you take a look at your background and begin to develop your personal identification, don't be limited by the chronological list of your experiences. Take a look at everything you have done and how even seemingly unrelated events might be of potential value.

A clear understanding of who you are right now is the first critical step in integrational processing. The work sheet at the end of this chapter is designed to lead you to that understanding.

Your Vision

The analysis of your current reality is only half of your personal identification. The other half, very simply put, is what you would like to do. This requires some creativity, and the easiest place to begin the creative process is at the end. In other words, you have to know where you want to end up before you can decide how to get there.

The best way to do this is to visualize your own funeral. There will be four speakers at the service: a family member, a friend, a professional associate, and an associate from your church or a community organization. What would you like these speakers to say about you and your life?

You might want to start thinking about that now, because it's a question you will encounter in the vision portion of the Personal Identification Work Sheet. And when you have a clear picture of how you want to be remembered, you'll be able to make each day a meaningful contribution to your life as a whole. You'll be certain that whatever you do does not violate or detract from the criteria you have defined as most important.

As you consider that, keep in mind that it is not necessary for your personal objectives to have anything to do with your personal history or professional experience. It is also not important, at this stage, for you to concern yourself with how you might achieve your vision. What is important is to understand very clearly and precisely what it is you want out of life.

A friend of mine, Tom, spent twenty years with the same corporation before he lost his job in a management shuffle. He was devastated. For four years he wallowed in a misery of his own making. He dabbled in a variety of activities that would seem interesting to most people, but that left him dissatisfied. He was bright and talented; he just couldn't seem to find a place for himself where he was comfortable. He couldn't find a substitute for the commitment he had made to his former employer.

He invited me to his home for dinner one evening, and our conversation naturally drifted to his floundering career. He complained of feeling stifled and frustrated.

I had been waiting for the opportunity to discuss integrational processing with him, and this seemed to be it. So I suggested quite casually that just for a moment he set aside all the pressures associated with making money and ignore considerations like practical skills and experience. Then I asked, "Tom, if it were your choice and you had no obstacles, if you could do anything you wanted to do, what would it be?"

He didn't have an answer for me that night. Several weeks later, he called and asked if we could get together. Over lunch at the Chinese restaurant across the street from my office, he told me that, after a great deal of serious thought, he had realized what he really wanted to do—and it didn't have anything to do with the type of business in which he had invested so much of his life.

Tom has worn a hearing aid since he was a youngster, and consequently has always been extremely sensitive to the challenges faced on a daily basis by the hearing impaired. What he really wanted to do was find a way to assist the hearing impaired to function more normally in our society. That was his personal mission statement. In the next chapter, you'll see how Tom was able to apply this to a business.

When you take the time to examine your personal commitments and do an honest evaluation of your vision for yourself, often what will emerge is something completely different from anything you have ever done in the past. Certainly that was the case for Ward Keller, who founded the Remuda Ranch Center for Anorexia and Bulimia. Ward's background as a successful entrepreneur in the support services industry made him an apparently unlikely candidate to found a residential treatment center for young women suffering from anorexia and bulimia. That is, unlikely only if you didn't know that his youngest daughter, Jena, was anorexic.

Ward and his wife bought an abandoned dude ranch in Wickenburg, Arizona, as a family residence in a desperate attempt to create a peaceful, healing environment for Jena. Her dramatic recovery fueled Ward's decision to turn the ranch into a treatment center for women with the same condition.

In contrast to Ward, Harriet McNear, an old acquaintance from a local social group I headed up for a time, had never thought about owning her own business; she was a single mother raising two children and had a successful career as a printing broker. When her health began to fail and conventional medicine was not helping, a friend introduced her to macrobiotics, which is a diet and lifestyle based on the philosophies of Oriental medicine. Harriet began feeling better; she had more energy and was enjoying life in a way she never had before. She decided to share what she had learned by starting Harriet's Kitchen, a whole foods cooking school. In addition to group classes, she offers private consultations to individuals and works with restaurants that want to develop healthier menus.

A lighter example of being guided by your own personal identification is that of sisters Karen and Lyn Mandelbaum, who both attended the Tyler School of Art in Philadelphia but found the life of a fine artist lacking in complete satisfaction. They wanted to create a business that would combine their art history education with a love of mystery, whimsy, and symbols of the past. The result was Island Magic Jewelry, a line of earrings and talisman necklaces sold in thousands of stores nationwide.

Tim Walsh wanted to play games for a living, so he came up with the idea of a board game and figured out how to turn it into a thriving business. His award-winning game, Tribond, is available in several versions and is distributed nationally.

While you are developing your personal identification, remember that profit potential doesn't matter at this level. What matters is understanding what's important to you, so you can build a business for yourself out of that knowledge.

How do you gain that understanding? By answering the questions in the Personal Identification Work Sheet at the end of this chapter.

After you have completed the work sheet, look for a pattern emerging from your answers. Are you using the skills and attributes you prefer, or are you allowing external forces to box you into a place where you don't want to be? By developing a clear, black-and-white picture of who you are right now—your current reality—you'll be prepared to take a look into the future so you can plan where you want to be tomorrow—your vision.

I have found that, in most cases, simply taking the time to work through this exercise will bring a level of clarity to your life that wasn't there before. By forcing yourself to articulate where you are now and where you would like to be, you have taken a major step toward getting there.

Your Personal Commitment Statement

You should now be able to take a look at your current reality, compare it with your vision, and define a personal commitment statement that reflects that vision.

What is your personal commitment statement? It's one sentence, no more than two lines long, that is a very specific description of what you're committed to do in your life. The reason for the length limitation is to keep you from rambling for a page or more. If your personal commitment statement takes more than one brief sentence, then you're not yet clear about what it is.

Tom's personal commitment was to assist the hearing-impaired to function more normally in our society. Harriet's was to help change the world for the better through diet. Tim's was to create a thinking game that would be fun to play.

Once your personal commitment statement is written, it needs to pass the following three tests:

(1) Is it clearly defined? The statement should be so clear that it is

easily communicable to someone else. If you read the sentence to someone else and they don't understand it, then you may not fully understand it yourself.

(2) Is it declaratory? The statement needs to be a forceful declaration. If it is subjunctive, like "If I had the chance to really go for it, and if everything goes okay, and if I get the opportunity, what I'd really like to do is . . . ," then it's not a personal commitment statement. A statement that reads, "What I intend to do is . . ." has power, and the ability to move you from where you are today to where you want to be tomorrow.

(3) Is it recognizable? When you achieve it, will you know it? When I travel from Orlando to Cleveland and I get to Cleveland, I know I'm there. I can recognize the city. If your personal commitment statement is not recognizable, it won't have the power you need. And the more recognizable and specific it is, the better. Wanting to go to Los Angeles is good. Wanting to go to the Espresso Cafe at the intersection of Pacific and Santa Monica Boulevard in Los Angeles is a whole lot better.

The more defined, the more declaratory, the more recognizable your personal commitment statement is, the more power it will have to move you from your current reality to your vision. If you're clear on where you are and you're clear on where you want to be, that statement will pull you forward in the right direction.

However, it's not necessary to carve this statement in granite. As you change and evolve over the years, so will your personal commitment statement. Things will happen to affect your perception of the world and your role in it. The key is to be sure that if you change your personal commitment statement, you do so only after serious and careful introspection, and you make the new statement clearly defined, declaratory, and recognizable.

Is a personal commitment statement absolutely essential to success? No. There are lots of successful business people who have never bothered to formally develop their personal identification or write a commitment statement. But it's been my experience that those who do will be more successful and have more fulfilling lives. Remember the buggy whips? If your product is targeted to the right market under the proper marketing premise, then your business is only a question of operating so you feel your efforts are worthwhile, not only for the marketplace, but also for yourself.

•   •   •

Two major things will come out of this analysis. The first is an in-depth understanding of your personal commitment, as evidenced by how you completed the life purpose statement. Notice that it is very similar to a business mission statement, which you will learn how to develop in the next chapter. This allows you to integrate your personal vision with how you manifest yourself in the business world. Unlike a job, entrepreneurism gives you the opportunity to do what you want to do and create what you want to create based on who you are, not based on the demands of an employer. Integrational processing lets you take advantage of that.

The second result of this analysis is that you now have the opportunity for momentum. You know who you are and where you would like to be. Now you can turn your attention to and invest your energy in a direction that transforms what could otherwise be a mundane job into a creative and profitable entrepreneurial pursuit.

What's more, you have applied a problem-solving process that you will use again and again, because it is adaptable to virtually any type of business or personal challenge you are ever likely to face.

The second step in integrational processing deals with your business identification, and we'll apply the same technique there that we did with your personal identification.

PERSONAL IDENTIFICATION WORK SHEET

CURRENT REALITY

The following will assist you in indentifying your current reality.

A. *List the five things you do best.*

    1.

    2.

    3.

4.

5.

B. *List the five things you do least well.*

1.

2.

3.

4.

5.

C. *List the five attributes of which you are most proud.*

1.

2.

3.

4.

5.

D. *List the five things of which you are least proud.*

1.

2.

3.

4.

5.

E. *List five things you do that you would like to stop doing.*

1.

2.

3.

4.

5.

F. *List five things about yourself and your life with which you are dissatisfied and which you would like to change.*

    1.

    2.

    3.

    4.

    5.

G. *List five things that continue to recur in your life even though you don't want them to.*

    1.

    2.

    3.

    4.

    5.

H. *What are your hobbies?*

    1.

    2.

    3.

    4.

    5.

I. *What do you enjoy most about your hobbies?*

    1.

    2.

    3.

    4.

    5.

J. *In what organizations do you hold memberships, and why?*

K. *What is your primary source of income at this time?*

L. *What would you like to change about your source of income?*

M. *Describe the home in which you currently live.*

N. *What would you like to change about your home?*

VISION

The function of the next series of questions is to aid you in identifying your vision or visions, and in creating priorities between and among them.

A. *List five things you would like to be remembered for when you die.*

    1.

    2.

    3.

    4.

    5.

B. *If you had five years to live, what would you concentrate on doing?*

    1.

    2.

    3.

    4.

    5.

    6.

    7.

    8.

    9.

    10.

C. *If you had three years to live, what would you concentrate on doing?*

    1.

    2.

    3.

    4.

    5.

D. *If you had one year to live, what would you concentrate on doing?*

_____

E. *Are you doing that now? If not, why not?*

_____

F. *List three things in descending order of importance that you have not yet proven about yourself, but would like to.*

    1.

    2.

    3.

G. *List three positive characteristics you haven't yet been acknowledged for having.*

    1.

    2.

    3.

H. *List three things you are that you haven't been acknowledged for being.*

    1.

    2.

    3.

I. *List ten things you want to do that you haven't done.*

1.

2.

3.

4.

5.

6.

7.

8.

9.

10.

J. *List ten things you want to be and are not.*

1.

2.

3.

4.

5.

6.

7.

8.

9.

10.

K. *List five things you want to be doing presently and are not doing.*

1.

2.

3.

4.

5.

Because your current reality reflects where you are at this moment and your vision reflects your objectives for the future, you should see a pattern emerging from this work sheet that tells you what your personal commitment is. This personal commitment is for yourself; it is not guided by profit, it is not guided by pragmatics. It is guided most specifically by your highest truth of where you see yourself best participating in the world.

Take a moment now to crystallize your personal commitment by completing the following sentence:

My personal commitment is to _____

_____

_____

Chapter One Highlights

—Integrational processing is a method of understanding yourself and your desires with the ultimate goal of identifying the right business and market for you.

—Personal identification is the first step in integrational processing. Begin by developing a clear understanding of where you are right now, which is your current reality, along with what you would like to see in the future, which is your vision.

—Your current reality includes all aspects of your life, not only those you normally associate with business.

—Your vision should not be concerned with how you will achieve it; it is only important at this point to know what you want.

—The answers to the Personal Identification Work Sheet will allow you to complete your personal commitment statement.

—To be effective, your personal commitment statement must be clearly defined, declaratory, and recognizable.

CHAPTER TWO

Business Identification
What Are You Running Here?

"The entrepreneur is essentially a visualizer and an actualizer
. . . He can visualize something, and when he visualizes it he
sees exactly how to make it happen."
—Robert L. Schwartz, Journalist

THE SECOND LEVEL of integrational processing is your business identification. As you did with your personal identification, you'll take a detailed look at your current reality and form a clear picture of where you would like your business to be in the future. The first part of integrational processing allowed you to create a personal commitment statement. When you complete the second part, you will have the information you need to develop a very specific and definitive business mission statement. We'll begin with an examination of your current reality.

If you are not presently in business, your current reality is simple: you don't have one. You have an empty slate to work with. But that doesn't mean you can skip this section of integrational processing. You still need to answer a few questions about your current reality before you can move on to your vision.

On the other hand, if you are in business right now, you need to take a look at your situation as it stands today. You need to examine your product or service line, your infrastructure, how you market—everything that relates to the current status of your business operation.

For the initial analysis, it's not important that you do anything more than identify the way things are. Don't worry about how things got that way, whether they are good or bad, or what you need to do to change them. Just develop a clear, clean understanding of your current business reality—that is, what is going on in your business *today*. I do this with each new case that comes into my law practice. I begin by analyzing the way things are, not by thinking about how I want them to be. To get the results I want, I must first understand the current reality.

Where Is Your Business Today?

When you develop a detailed portrait of what your business looks like today, you can decide whether or not that is what you want. You do that by contrasting your current reality with your vision. And if you do not have a concise, definitive business mission statement, integrational processing will help you develop one. Whatever your business objectives are, this much is absolutely true: there is no successful business that does not have a very specific mission statement.

When Chuck Givens created the Charles J. Givens Organization, his business intention was "to create the largest financial education institution in the country." He did.

When Bill Gates and Paul Allen founded Microsoft Corp., their mission was "A computer on every desk and in every home, all running Microsoft software." Antitrust laws may make the literal achievement of this goal impossible, but this billion-dollar company offers the broadest array of products in the personal computer software business.

When Mo Siegel started Celestial Seasonings, his mission was "to provide a very high quality herb tea in beautiful packaging at a good price to as wide a distribution as possible." Siegel's achievements were attractive enough that Kraft was willing to pay about $25 million for Celestial Seasonings when the company was only twelve years old.

The mission statement is what propels your business forward. Once you have identified your business's current reality, you can decide if that reality reflects exactly what it is you want to do. If the reality is point A, and your business vision is point B, your business mission will be the vehicle that moves you between those two points. Out of your personal statement came a personal commitment; out of your business statement will come a business mission. And all you've done to achieve this is look internally.

Keep in mind that the principles of integrational processing do not have any geographic restrictions, but it's possible your business will. That's why the answers to the first two questions in the current reality section are important. Your business or idea may be better suited for a locale different from where you are now, but if your obligations prevent you from moving, you've got some challenges to work out.

Stan, a former student of mine, owned a sporting goods store in a small fishing village in Alaska. When he attended one of my seminars, he told me point-blank that my theories sounded great, but he didn't see what he could do to apply them in his current location. I don't remember our conversation verbatim, but it went something like this:

ME: Is your reality the fact that you're in a small fishing village in Alaska?

STAN: Yes.

ME: Is your reality the fact that there is only a population of approximately eleven hundred people who are capable of buying sporting goods and fishing equipment from you?

STAN: Yes.

ME: So that's part of your current reality. Is there any way you can move out of Alaska?

STAN: No, my entire family and my wife's family are here.

ME: So is it a fair statement to say you're pretty much stuck in Alaska?

STAN: That's right.

ME: So that's also part of your current reality. Instead of treating the fact that you're in Alaska as a liability, why don't you turn it into an asset? Use it in a way that will give you the opportunity to build something successful. Let me ask you something, Stan. Where is L. L. Bean located?

STAN: I'm not sure. I think it's somewhere in New England.

ME: That's right. They're in Freeport, Maine. Do you know what the population of Freeport, Maine, is?

STAN: No.

ME: Do you care what the population of Freeport, Maine, is?

STAN: No.

ME: Of course not. When you look at the L. L. Bean catalog, or any other catalog, do you ask them what the population is of the city or town they are headquartered in?

STAN: No.

ME: When you look at their merchandise, do you ask them whether they're stuck in that town, or if they could move if they wanted to, or, for that matter, how much merchandise they sell to locals?

STAN: No.

ME: Do you care at all about anything except their marketing message and the merchandise they are presenting to you?

STAN: I guess not.

ME: Right. So let me ask you this: Where is Banana Republic located? Where is Sharper Image located?

STAN: I don't know.

ME: When you receive a copy of either of their catalogs, do you care where the merchandise is being shipped from?

STAN: Not really.

ME: So if you were to market a particular type of fishing gear, and you establish a premium based on the fact it's Alaskan fishing gear used in an area known worldwide for its sport fishing, do you think for a second that anybody is going to care that you happen to be located in some tiny little fishing village in Alaska rather than a major metropolitan area? In fact, couldn't that be developed into a marketing asset?

STAN: I see your point.

ME: I'm glad you do. Your current reality is not something that has to be a liability. Don't beat yourself over the head with it. Appraise it objectively, because from your current reality will come not only limitations but also opportunities for how you're going to create your business operation. I see a lot of marketing benefits for gear that has weathered the Alaskan fishing season and is thus obviously capable of enduring lake fishing in the central part of the United States.

Stan did not say another word for the rest of the seminar, but he took about thirty-five pages of notes.

The point is, don't be judgmental as you outline your current reality. Your purpose with this exercise is simply to observe the way things are right now. When you judge, you limit yourself. When you observe, you create opportunities.

It's also important to have a clear picture of your own financial circumstances. What resources do you have? How long could you survive without income? Do you have assets to offer as collateral for a loan? Even though I have said that under-capitalization takes the rap for many business failures when in fact the problem was simply that the business was wrong for the entrepreneur involved, the truth is you do need some capital. It's important that you understand what you have and how much you'll need to get your business going.

If the answer to the question "Do you currently own a business?" is no, you're ready to move ahead with developing a detailed picture of your vision for the future. If you currently own a business, take the time to understand its role in your life and how well it is meeting your needs. Without this basic knowledge, you will be unable to formulate a plan that will allow you to make adjustments to provide for greater satisfaction and success.

Picture Your Business Tomorrow

The vision portion of the Business Identification Work Sheet will provide you with the information you need to create the company you truly want. Most entrepreneurs are motivated by a desire for financial and creative independence, but those are broad concepts which need to be refined to be useful. Besides, the true underlying issue here is *not* financial independence. Any business operated well will give you financial independence. For the same reason, the issue is also not profit. Conduct your business according to certain well-defined parameters, and you will be profitable.

The issue is whether that business is going to provide personal satisfaction, the lifestyle you truly want, and a product or service line that satisfies you to the depths of your being.

If you're going to develop a true business identification, you must know your business's personality, both as it exists now and as you plan for it to be, as well as you do your own. Once you do, you'll be able to develop a business mission statement.

Earlier I talked about Chuck Givens's business mission statement: to create the largest financial education institution in the country. Chuck was able to write that mission statement because he had a clear understanding of his current reality and his vision, and that was apparent to me from the first day I met him.

When I was first contacted about teaching for the Givens Organization, it was by a recruiter who was looking for someone who was knowledgeable about business and finance, who was also an investor, and who could teach that material to other people. After some preliminary meetings, the recruiter took me out to meet Chuck.

At that time, Chuck was operating out of a house in Winter Springs, a middle-income "bedroom community" adjacent to Orlando. The house was a small, plain building—certainly not the home or office of anyone's dreams. But what really struck me as we pulled up was the sign outside.

It was huge.

It was bigger than the house itself, and it read, "Charles J. Givens Foundation." Literally, you couldn't see the building for the sign.

We went inside, and I was not particularly impressed with the ambience. Books were stacked to the ceiling. The metal furniture looked like something you would find in an Army surplus store. (As a matter of fact, I found out later it *was* from an Army surplus store.) Chuck was in shirtsleeves, and his staff at the time totaled six people.

I began our conversation by asking what he was all about. His answer was short and to the point. He said, "My intention is to create the largest financial education institution in the country."

It was immediately obvious that this was a person who had a very clear and keen sense of what his position was going to be in the financial history of this country. It was also obvious that the house was Chuck's current reality, but the sign—that huge, overwhelming sign announcing the Charles J. Givens Foundation—was his vision.

Just as your personal commitment statement needs to pass the three tests of declaration, clarity, and recognizability, so does your business mission statement. Did Chuck's statement pass those three tests? I'm sure you can answer that for yourself. Are you at all confused about his intention? I certainly wasn't.

Did Chuck say, "If I can get some financing, and if I get a few breaks, I want to build a large financial education organization"? Not at all. He said, "My intention is to create the largest financial education institution in the country."

Was there any possibility I would not understand his intention? No. It was very declaratory and very clear. It was also totally recognizable.

When I was in Chuck's office a few years later, he tossed a newspaper across the desk to me. It carried the announcement that one of the financial gurus had gone bankrupt. Chuck leaned back in his chair and said, "The Givens Organization is now the largest financial education institution in the country." He had achieved a plainly recognizable position.

When June Morris decided to start an airline, her mission was to get more people traveling by air. She believed that if fares were affordable, people who would not otherwise fly would do so. The success and profitability of Morris Air proved she was right. For example, during the first quarter Morris Air offered service between Oakland, California, and Salt Lake City, Utah, the market expanded by approximately 46,000 passengers—that is, 46,000 more tickets were sold for that route than had been sold in previous periods. And she had done the same thing on route after route.

Obviously, June's mission met the test of being declaratory, clear, and recognizable. She didn't waffle around or prepare excuses in case she failed. "We're very focused," she said. "From the day we started, our goal was to make travel affordable to people who were not traveling. By doing that, we were able to expand the market enormously for our own airline and for the other carriers."

Model your own business mission statement after these. Make it clearly communicable, easy to understand, and something you will recognize when you achieve it. When a business mission statement is both concise and precise, it offers the power to draw you from your current reality to where you want to be.

Let me stress the importance of completing the personal identification section before you work on your business identification. Your personal commitment statement is to your personal identification what your business mission statement is to your business identification. That may sound like a complicated algebraic formula, but it's not. Both your personal commitment statement and your business mission statement allow you to move from your current reality to your vision based on an understanding of who you are and how you would like to project yourself to the outside world.

By developing both a personal and a business identification, you will be equipped to make a decision on how you will professionally manifest your skills and talents in terms of your personal vision. If you are currently in business, you will realize just how closely your business reflects your personal identification and what you need to do to make the two consistent and compatible.

Remember, this is a time to continue the introspection you began in Chapter One. Don't concern yourself at this point with the outside world. That will keep until you've discovered who you really are and what business will best meet your needs. Once you have done that, you'll be ready for the third step of integrational processing: your market identification.

BUSINESS IDENTIFICATION WORK SHEET

CURRENT REALITY

The following questions will assist you in clearly identifying your business's current circumstances.

A. *Where do you live?*

B. *How long, if at all, will you be required to live there?*

C. *Describe your current economic picture.*

> **1.** If you are employed, what is your current salary?
>
> **2.** List all of your income sources.
>
> **3.** List your liquid assets.
>
> **4.** List your nonliquid assets.

D. *Do you currently own a business?*

E. *If so:*

> **1.** What is its purpose?
>
> **2.** What is its product?

3. What is its market?

4. What reputation does it have in the marketplace?

5. Does it satisfy your personal objectives?

6. In what ways does it represent what you want to be doing?

7. In what ways does it fail to represent what you want to be doing?

8. How do you market?

9. Do you operate from a home office or commercial space?

10. Do you require a warehouse? If so, what type?

11. Do you have employees? If so, list their names, job titles, and a brief description of what they do.

12. List the office equipment (e.g., typewriters, computers, calculators, telephones) you own.

13. List the product equipment you own.

14. Do you have a satisfied customer base?

15. Is your business producing what you want to produce?

VISION

The function of the following questions is to assist you in identifying your business vision or visions and in creating priorities between and among them.

A. *List the five attributes of your business of which you are or would be most proud.*

1.

2.

3.

4.

5.

B. *List five possible changes you would like to make in your current business.*

    1.

    2.

    3.

    4.

    5.

C. *If you could be known for three main business accomplishments, what would you like them to be?*

    1.

    2.

    3.

D. *List five attributes of your business of which you are or would be least proud.*

    1.

    2.

    3.

    4.

    5.

E. *List three aspects you would most enjoy in the business life you want to have.*

    1.

    2.

    3.

F. *If you overheard a conversation about your business between two strangers, what would you like for them to say?*

    1.

    2.

    3.

4.

5.

G. *If you overheard two of your best friends or most cherished relatives talking about your business, what would you like for them to say?*

1.

2.

3.

4.

5.

H. *Describe what your life would look like if you were involved in the business of your choice.*

Just as you compared your personal current reality with your personal vision to develop a personal commitment, you have now examined where you are in terms of your business right now and then articulated where you would like to be in the future. Again, you are not concerned with profit. You are looking deep within yourself for a vision of your business ideal.

With this mental picture, you are now prepared to make a commitment for your business by completing the following statement:

The purpose of my business is to _____

_____

_____

Chapter Two Highlights

—The second step in integrational processing is your business identification. This involves a clear understanding of where you are right now in terms of your business and what you would like for the future to hold.

—Your current reality includes geographic and financial specifics. If you are currently in business, take a very close look at your operation and the satisfaction it offers you.

—Your vision is a well-defined picture of what you want. Don't concern yourself at this point with how you plan to achieve it; simply understand it in detail.

—The answers to the Business Identification Work Sheet will allow you to complete your business mission statement.

—To be effective, your business mission statement must be clearly defined, declaratory, and recognizable.

CHAPTER THREE

Market Identification
Whom Do You Want to Serve?

"If you want to succeed you should strike out on new paths
rather than travel the worn paths of accepted success."

—John D. Rockefeller

YOUR MISSION STATEMENT springs from an inner desire to meet deep, personal needs, but your business decisions must be grounded in the reality of the marketplace. Now that you have taken the time to understand what is important to you personally and how you can extend that to the outside world in the form of a profit-making business operation, you are ready for the third step of integrational processing. You now must determine to what specific position in the marketplace you will best be able to adapt your particular business.

For myself, the process went like this:

My personal commitment statement is "To create the conditions in which successful and effective living will be available for everyone." From that, I developed a business mission statement that says, "My business mission is to provide opportunities for individuals to learn to become more successful and effective in their lives."

In creating those two statements, I wasn't concerned with how I was going to accomplish my mission. I knew that if I understood where I was and had a clear vision of where I wanted to be, the market would tell me how to get there.

What the market ultimately told me was that adults needed strong and rigorous education in areas associated with self-employment opportunities. The existing seminar industry simply did not produce the quality of education necessary for adults to learn seriously how to produce income for themselves in this day and age. That perception formed the foundation of my company, The Open University.

I have done a lot of other things in my life. I was successful in the sporting goods business; I have owned a number of profitable restaurants; my law practice has always been extremely profitable. But none of those things could possibly compare to the personal satisfaction that I have received in growing The Open University Company, stretching into the marketplace based one hundred percent on my own personal commitment.

What will the market tell you? You will find out by applying the same principles of integrational processing that you did in the two previous chapters.

The Market As It Is Today

Your business mission statement provides a circle that allows opportunities for examination of the marketplace, and that circle encompasses certain players. It is those players we want to study next.

It might help you to think of the marketplace as a football field. If there's a 250-pound center guard firmly entrenched on the fifty-yard line, that's not where you want to be. You don't need to fight that center guard for his space; instead, find a place that's not occupied and claim it for your own.

It doesn't matter if the playing field has one hundred or five hundred or just ten players on it—the analogy is the same. You want to find the turf that is not currently occupied by an existing player.

Understand that players are not necessarily competitors. In fact, this analysis of existing players in your marketplace will help you eliminate competition (we'll discuss that in more detail in the next chapter). So look around you. Who's playing on your field?

When Chuck Givens determined that his mission was to create an institution to teach financial subjects, he considered all the organizations that were providing services similar to what was included in his business mission statement. He took a look at the circle of players out there, which included Fred Pryor, Al Lowry, Mark O. Haroldsen, Robert Allen, Dave Del Dotto, CareerTrack, and others. That was the current reality of the marketplace for Chuck.

When Rebecca Matthias decided to start Mother's Work, a company specializing in maternity wear for career women, she first identified the other players: specialty stores, major maternity chains, boutiques, and maternity departments in major stores. For Ward Keller, the other players offering treatment for girls with eating disorders were psychiatric facilities with short-term programs. For June Morris, the other players were large, established airlines, regional carriers, and charter services.

Your first step in developing your market identification is to identify the players on the field—know who is out there and what they're doing.

Your next step is to identify the similarities and differences among the players. Understand why they are in their particular positions. This will give you the information you need to take your own place on the field.

Look for similarities in product, marketing techniques, production, distribution, and operations. These are all players on the same field, so they will have some common characteristics. Note what they are.

Once you've compared the players for sameness, contrast them to discover their differences. You might find that one player sells the same product retail that another sells by mail order. For example, Office Depot is a retail discount office products chain; Quill offers discount office products by mail order. Same product, different distribution.

The difference might be in the marketing method. As an independent computer retailer, CDS Computers doesn't buy paid advertising. Computerland, a national chain, invests heavily in broadcast and print ads. Same product, different marketing method.

There may be some basic differences in product. The field of players may all be in the seminar business, but Mark O. Haroldsen teaches real estate and Fred Pryor does middle management courses—definitely a different product. Hilton Hotels and Scottish Inns are both lodging chains, but the amenities offered by a Hilton make a stay at one of their hotels quite a different product from a stay in the rooms offered by Scottish Inns.

So clarify your playing field. Note where every player is, both horizontally and vertically, in all aspects of the business. There's no point in getting into the game until you've done this.

As you conduct your analysis, keep this in mind: some people have a natural tendency to want to show they can do something better than someone else, and indeed you may be able to do just that. But rather than worrying about doing anything better, concern yourself instead with doing something different.

It is differentness, not betterness, that means success in business.

It certainly won't hurt if, as you examine the other players, you develop a clear evaluation of what they are doing wrong. Take advantage of the learning opportunity presented by their mistakes. But the most important issue of this exercise is *not* right or wrong, better or worse—it is *difference*. Remember, the other players are players because they have identified a market that allows them to do whatever it is they do for that market. If they weren't doing something right, they wouldn't be in business and you wouldn't need to concern yourself with them. So assume they are doing something right, but decide what could be different.

Once you have compared and contrasted all the other players, it's time to ask yourself the fundamental question: what makes you different from them?

You need to know not only what makes the other players different from each other, but also what is going to set you apart from them. Recognize that your mission statement has already told the world what field you intend to occupy. Now you are creating differences between yourself and the other players in that field.

When Chuck Givens examined the other players, he found a group of seminar leaders who taught real estate, a group who taught investments, a group who taught management, and a group who taught career programs. There was no one out there teaching total financial education. So out of the differences between and the similarities among the relevant players in the market, what distinguished Chuck emerged as "Money Strategies for the 80s," a total financial education program that formed the foundation for his organization today.

Rebecca Matthias found that major maternity chains specialized in casual, lower-priced fashions and the selection in other stores was limited. Shunning retail in favor of a broader mail-order market, she put together a catalog of maternity clothes appropriate for career situations and developed a strategy targeting professional women in the early stages of pregnancy. Today, Mothers Work is a multimillion-dollar manufacturing and retail company with stores across the country.

Ward Keller realized most psychiatric hospitals offered a thirty-day program focusing on curing the symptoms rather than the underlying cause of anorexia and bulimia. So the Remuda Ranch offers group and individual therapy; classes on nutrition, addiction, and women's issues; plus an innovative equestrian program, where patients are paired with horses for the duration of their stay. Giving patients the responsibility for the love, care, and well-being of an animal contributes to the development of confidence and self-esteem, and sets the Remuda Ranch apart from all other facilities with eating-disorder treatment units.

Eric, a client of mine, was fascinated by lasers and wanted to start a business in the laser industry. He had a list of players a mile long. There were lasers for medical use, for research, for construction. There were optical lasers and industrial lasers; lasers that scanned and lasers that cut.

If Eric had defined a market niche for himself that pitted him against any of these companies, it would have meant starting out with that many competitors. So, instead, he decided to manufacture lasers designed for fingerprint detection and analysis for law enforcement agencies. Since no other company was doing that, he created a market niche where he had no competition.

It is from the field of relevant players that you will define your competition, and that definition determines whether you will be competing against dozens of other companies or operating comfortably in a class by yourself. The market identification portion of integrational processing lets you establish a market niche that differentiates you from all the other players. From there, you create a market that is yours alone to dominate.

Your Company As It Will Be in the Future

After you've identified the players and compared and contrasted them, the difference between you and those other players ultimately becomes your vision of the future for yourself and your market.

For your personal identification, it's *commitment;* for your business identification, it's *mission;* and for market identification, it's *market position.* You create your position in the marketplace, and if it's a place no one else is occupying, you have no competitors.

It's only when you misperceive your market that you end up in a battle over turf. It's so much easier just to create a space that's comfortably your own.

Let me stress that well-defined market niches rarely happen by accident; they are created in advance. Once you understand your own current reality and have taken an objective look at the relevant players in your business area, you can begin to consider the position in the marketplace that will be most appropriate for you. It is only after you have researched the market that you can determine the best niche for your company and develop a market position statement for it.

That statement will naturally build on your personal commitment statement and your business mission statement, and will clearly say where you intend to position your company. Banana Republic makes an excellent market position statement by producing and selling natural fabric clothing with a wilderness or safari theme. There is also no doubt about the market position of The Sharper Image: they distribute high-tech products that are otherwise difficult to obtain.

When you have written your market position statement, test it as you did your personal commitment and business mission statements for declaration, clarity, and recognizability.

Now That You Know Where You Want to Go

Once you have completed the three steps involved in integrational processing, you should be sharply focused on a business operation that is right for you. The process is very much like an inverted triangle: your personal identification and commitment are based on the broad circumstances of heredity, environment, and experience. Your business identification is more narrow, with a mission statement that clearly defines your goals and purpose. With market identification, you are able to target defined groups of prospective customers who are likely to purchase your product or service.

After my friend Tom began his own adventure with integrational processing by developing a personal commitment to assist the hearing-impaired to function more normally in our society, he went on to create a business that would do just that. He started a company to distribute products compatible with his personal commitment, which gave him his business mission statement.

He researched the market and discovered that there was no product available to help the hearing-impaired with an everyday problem. At that time, when hearing aid wearers watched television or listened to the radio, they could do one of two things. They could turn up the

Personal I.D.
_____

Business I.D.

_____

Market I.D.

Illustration of inverted triangle

hearing aid, which would amplify the sound of the programming, but would also amplify the sound of everything else in the room, including the newspaper shuffling, the dog barking, the pots and pans rattling, and so forth. Or they could turn up the volume on the television or stereo, and blast everyone else out of the room. Neither option was particularly satisfying.

Tom studied the situation and determined that it could be resolved electronically. He found an electronics manufacturer to build the product: a small wireless transmitter designed to be attached to the back of a television or stereo, and a lightweight headset receiver. The volume on the headset could be adjusted to a level comfortable for the wearer without disturbing anyone else in the room. A bonus for Tom was that not only could the hearing-impaired benefit, but the product had a strong consumer application as well. If one person in a household wanted to watch television, but no one else did, they could use the headset. And because it was wireless, the wearer could move around the house without missing any dialogue.

For Tom, what began as an examination of his personal identification ended up as an extremely profitable business operation. That transmitter turned out to be just one item in a catalog of products he designed to assist the hearing-impaired. Tom was able to take his personal commitment, create a business mission statement, and position himself favorably in the market.

Integrational processing provides a structure for you to use in creating a profitable business operation that is, on a day-to-day basis, satisfying and appropriate for your personal considerations and commitments. Having found your niche, it's time to begin building your company.

MARKET IDENTIFICATION WORK SHEET

CURRENT REALITY

To create your market niche, begin by accurately portraying the reality of the marketplace. The following questions will assist you.

A. *List those businesses that share some aspects of your business purpose.*

    1.

    2.

    3.

    4.

    5.

B. *How are they the same?*

    1.

    2.

    3.

    4.

    5.

C. *How are they different?*

    1.

    2.

    3.

    4.

    5.

D. *For each one, state specifically*

    1. What appears to be the primary value added—that is, the value to the consumer—of the business's product(s) or service(s)?

        a.

        b.

        c.

        d.

        e.

2. What products or services does each one produce or distribute?

    a.

    b.

    c.

    d.

    e.

3. How do they distribute?

    a.

    b.

    c.

    d.

    e.

4. How do they market?

    a.

    b.

    c.

    d.

    e.

5. How do they produce?

    a.

    b.

    c.

    d.

    e.

6. What makes the way each produces, markets, or distributes unique?

    a.

    b.

    c.

    d.

    e.

E. *Do these businesses satisfy the entire market? Why or why not?*

_____

_____

_____

F. *What does that tell you about what may or may not be needed?*

    1.

    2.

    3.

    4.

    5.

G. *What areas of the market consistent with your business purpose are being filled?*

    1.

    2.

    3.

    4.

    5.

VISION

The following questions will assist you in identifying the best position in the marketplace for you to assume.

A. *List in descending order of priority five areas of the marketplace that are not being satisfied at this time.*

    1.

    2.

    3.

    4.

    5.

B. *Why not?*

    1.

    2.

    3.

    4.

    5.

C. *What other areas of the market consistent with your purpose need attention?*

    1.

    2.

    3.

    4.

    5.

D. *List in descending order what appear to you to be the five least touched areas of the marketplace?*

    1.

    2.

    3.

    4.

    5.

E. *List in descending order which areas of the marketplace are most closely aligned with your talents and skills.*

    1.

    2.

    3.

    4.

    5.

F. *List in descending order which areas would be the easiest to identify and to target.*

    1.

    2.

    3.

    4.

    5.

G. *List in descending order the areas which can be tapped most efficiently.*

    1.

    2.

    3.

    4.

    5.

H. *Which areas consistently appear in your answers D through G?*

1.

2.

3.

I. *Do you have special circumstances that tend to favor or disfavor a particular area? If so, which and why?*

J. What do you see as that area's critical function?

The key to finding your market niche is understanding both your own market and the other players on the field so well that you can define a position for yourself that no one else is occupying—a unique position that allows you to eliminate competition. Now that you have determined your current market reality by closely examining all the companies sharing some aspect of your business purpose, and have developed a clear vision of your own market, you can complete the following statement:

My market position statement is _____

_____

_____

Chapter Three Highlights

—The third step in integrational processing is your market identification. This involves a clear understanding of the market and an in-depth analysis of the players in your area of interest.

—Visualize the market as a playing field and choose a location for yourself that is not occupied by anyone else.

—The answers to the Market Identification Work Sheet will allow you to develop a market position statement.

—Your market position statement should pass the tests of clear definition, declaration, and recognizability.

CHAPTER FOUR

What Business Is All About
Putting the Horse Before the Cart

"The more people who own little businesses of their own, the safer our country will be, and the better off its cities and towns; for the people who have a stake in their country and their community are its best citizens."

—John Hancock

WHEN I WAS IN COLLEGE, I was a fencer, and the way we trained provided me with the seeds that ultimately grew into the basic principles of integrational processing. We didn't start out slashing our fencing foils through the air in the hopes of hitting a target. Quite the contrary: it was some time before we were even allowed to pick up a foil. We began by practicing the proper posture, and extending our arms with our fingers pointed. The next step, still without the foil, was to work on, with our arms and fingers extended, hitting a tennis ball that was suspended from the ceiling on a string.

Once we were able to consistently hit the tennis ball with our fingers, we were allowed to hold the foil. We still weren't allowed to fence with it, but we could hold it. In fact, I carried that foil with me every-where I went—to class, to the library, to the dining hall, to the showers—literally everywhere, always using the correct posture.

It didn't matter where I pointed the foil; I could point it anywhere. But it had become a part of me, a natural extension of my arm.

Finally, the instructors said we could try hitting something with the foil. We went back to the tennis balls hanging from the ceiling. We would extend our foils and lunge. Sometimes we hit the ball, sometimes we missed it. But we tried repeatedly, until the instructors decided we were ready for another challenge: they started moving the ball. We had to try to hit balls that sometimes rotated in a predictable pattern and other times swung in a totally haphazard and unpredictable motion.

When we became skilled at hitting that moving tennis ball with the foil, we were ready to fence.

The steps in learning to fence parallel the steps of integrational processing. First you determine who you are, and extend your arm, comfortable with its direction (your personal identification). Then you create a business (your business identification) that is literally an extension of yourself, as the foil is an extension of the fencer's arm. With practice, you learn to point that foil, lunge, and hit your target. In business, your target is the market you have defined for yourself (your market identification). When you are able to consistently hit that market, you will build a very profitable company.

Learning to succeed in business is no different from learning how to fence. Fully integrated, the fencer and the businessperson stay focused and on target.

In addition, by completing the steps of integrational processing, you also identify six major by-products of the exercise—interlocking fundamentals that build on one another as you turn your vision into reality: focus, momentum, market niche, market dominance, elimination of competition, and structuring your business operation. Let's look at them one at a time.

Focus

Until such time as you create a market position for yourself, you have no purpose for being in business. As one of the by-products of integrational processing, focus allows your business to move in a particular direction. All too often when businesses fail, it is not for lack of talent, or for lack of capital, but simply because they were not focused. You cannot serve more than one master. By creating a market position and making that position a target, you will be focused.

Let me tell you about Softlab, a computer software company I was involved with. One of my partners, Chris, is a software genius. When he was nineteen, he created the software that helped NASA put a man on the moon. To say he is technically brilliant is an understatement.

The third partner in this operation, Kathy, is also brilliant, but her expertise is in administration and management. It appeared to be an unbeatable combination of skills and talent. But, as you probably know, things aren't always what they seem.

It was evident from the start that there were going to be some major problems.

Chris wanted a very highly specialized software development firm. He wanted to be part of a company that stayed on the cutting edge of technology in terms of producing products. His vision of the company was one with three or four other "techies" like himself doing research and developing innovative software packages.

Kathy, on the other hand, wanted a sales organization. She wanted a company that would combine hardware with software and sell it on a national level. She didn't want six people, she wanted sixteen people, and she wanted all of them out on the road selling.

I just wanted the whole thing to be profitable.

We live and learn. At the end of four years, the only thing Chris and Kathy had accomplished was to buy themselves mediocre salaries. As talented as they both were, they should have been earning five or six times as much. But that wasn't going to happen until the company was focused, and the company couldn't get focused until Chris and Kathy stopped pulling it in two different directions.

They finally realized that their differences were irreconcilable. Chris left the company and headed out west, where he found a niche that would allow him to do what he wanted and was comfortable with, and Kathy focused on other pursuits.

By using integrational processing to become focused, you can create a business and a market position that is independent of any of the other players on the field. Moreover, focus lets you concentrate on what will satisfy you. Focus does more than tell you what you're going to do; it tells you what you are *not* going to do. It allows you to rid yourself of distractions and disruptions as you point all your efforts and resources in one direction.

Momentum

Once you are focused, the momentum will build. Before Chuck Givens decided to build the largest financial educational institution in the country, he was traveling to just a few cities, he couldn't get on any local talk shows, and the newspapers wouldn't mention his name. But once he became focused, things began to move.

You've probably seen dramatic scenes in movies where the protagonist pushes his way through a crowd of obstacles, ignoring everything except his goal, to get to the prize—whatever that prize happens to be. That's how it was for Chuck when he developed a clear focus on what he wanted. He traveled to more and more cities, where local talk shows were delighted to have him as a guest. The leading daily papers began quoting him regularly. From there, he was able to move to network television. He's appeared with Sally Jessy Raphael and Phil Donahue, and he's been a regular on NBC's *Today*. Chuck has been featured in articles in national business, financial, and general publications. This has all come with the momentum that builds with focus.

Chuck was successful at every endeavor he pursued consistent with his primary mission statement. When his efforts departed from that primary mission, they were not successful. He had an interest in a football team, an indoor soccer team, a modeling agency, a castle in France, a restaurant, a printing company—all absolute disasters. When, and only when, Chuck was focused, he built momentum and succeeded. The same principle applies to you.

Delorise, a professional associate of mine, was one of the finest recruiters I have ever met. She could match up the right person to the right job with uncanny accuracy. As a matter of fact, I routinely turned to her to fill my human resource needs.

Her problem, however, was her inability to stay focused. She recruited for a few months, then got involved in property leasing for a while, then switched to investing, then came back to recruiting, until something else captured her attention.

With her talent and skill, Delorise could have created one of the top recruiting companies in the area, but she did not stay focused. Consequently, her professional and financial circumstances stayed the same for years, until she finally married and settled into her husband's work with a ministry.

Without directed momentum, your business will die. How can you actually arrive at any destination if you are going in several directions at once? It's like driving down the highway and having to make a turn every time you start to pick up speed. Every time you change direction, you have to slow down. There's no way you can build any real momentum.

But with focus, you will constantly build momentum and move toward a goal defined by your market identification.

Market Niche

Small business is not about business, it is about developing a market niche. A business without a market niche is not a business at all. It's nothing more than a substitute for earning a salary.

If you do not clearly define your position in the market, your resources will be diluted and the competition will be coming at you from every angle. You might limp along and earn yourself a living, and you might do as well as if you had a job working for someone else, but your business will not be truly successful.

As you learned when you were developing your market identification, the key is to find yourself a place on the field where no one else is.

In 1984, Tim Fisher and David Goldsmith studied the market and realized no one was specializing in providing communications equipment on a rental basis to the film, entertainment, and convention industries. People who needed such equipment generally turned to a rental service that specialized in lighting or camera equipment. Tim and David decided to position their company, CP Communications, in a place no one else occupied: as specialists in the communications equipment rental business. They could have targeted a number of other markets where other companies were already performing well, but they chose not to. CP Communications has grown into a multimillion-dollar company because Tim and David found their own market niche—one they could easily dominate.

Market Dominance

The idea that market dominance is a concept of big business is a myth. For a number of reasons, not the least of which is government interference, large companies have great difficulty creating market dominance. This concept is actually more appropriate and more important to small businesses.

Once you are focused and begin building momentum toward a particular market niche, you have created the very real possibility of dominating the market. Market dominance is to profitability what market niche is to business: in business, you must have a market niche; for profitability, you must have market dominance.

If you have the only Jewish delicatessen or the only Oriental food market within a ten-mile radius, you have market dominance. When my friend Tom started his catalog company with products for the hearing-impaired, he had market dominance.

A student in one of my early small business seminars wanted to turn her hobby of calligraphy into a business. Miriam had been addressing wedding invitations for friends and making a little money, but she needed a larger volume to make her hobby a self-supporting enterprise. When she asked the stationery and bridal departments of the fine department stores in her area if they could recommend a calligrapher to address envelopes, they couldn't. Her business was born.

With a brochure and rate sheet, she visited each major department store in the area. The stores were delighted to have an additional service to offer, and also delighted to have an additional source of profit, because they mark up Miriam's fees before they bill their customers. Miriam picks up the invitations and the guest list, goes home and does the work, and returns the completed product to the store. She works on a comfortable schedule, doing something she enjoys tremendously, and she *dominates her market*.

There are a lot of people who do calligraphy; there are a few who do it for money; but there is no one else in Miriam's area who provides to major department stores the service of addressing envelopes for wedding invitations. She has dominated her market by defining a niche so precise that there is no competition. Her annual income, by the way, is in the six figures.

It is only logical that if you have a clearly defined market niche and you are the only company occupying that niche, then you will have market dominance.

Understand that momentum is to focus what market dominance is to market niche: natural evolution.

Elimination of Competition

Can you really eliminate the competition? You bet you can. Do you do it by beating them? No, you do it by never fighting them in the first place. I call it sidestepping the fight.

There is nothing inherent in business that requires competition. On the contrary, it's smart to eliminate competition, and you do that by defining who you are and refining yourself away from all the other players. Through the market identification portion of integrational processing, you are able to establish a market niche that no one else shares. The more defined and precise your niche is, the easier it will be for you to establish a market that is yours alone.

When you look at your field, you'll see a lot of different types of players. If your niche is a circle, and you make that circle a big one and draw it around a lot of players, you'll have that many companies to compete against. Make your circle smaller and draw it around fewer players, and you'll only have a few companies to compete against. Make it even smaller, reflecting your own special market, and you have no competitors.

The extent to which you can create your own space on the field, to which you capture your own turf, is the extent to which you eliminate competition.

The same principle applies in politics. There is nothing to be gained by running against an incumbent, because you can't beat an incumbent. Certainly not every incumbent who chooses to run again is reelected, but it's not because they are defeated. Incumbents might lose, but you won't beat them. They might lose because they were stashing public money into their own pockets, or sleeping around, or lying to their constituents, or found to have shady business dealings, or indicted for a crime. Incumbents can do a lot of things to cause voters to elect a challenger, but they can't be beaten by an outsider unless they lose the race themselves.

Savvy politicians don't run against an incumbent; they run for an open seat, where the turf is empty.

Savvy business owners don't compete against an established player with a market share; they create a niche that is uniquely their own. So sidestep the fight—you can invest your energy in more profitable ways.

Once you have created and settled into your niche, you don't need to worry about competitors moving onto your turf, because the market—*your* market—identifies you with the product or service you're offering. All you need to do now is find more and more people who fall within that market.

But you must stay focused on your market niche.

Miriam's impressive success with her calligraphy business prompted her to consider selling calligraphy pens and stationery supplies. But as a calligrapher addressing invitations for upscale department stores, she had no competition. As a seller of pens, pencils, and paper, she would have had to compete against every art, office, and stationery supply store in town—as well as the very customers she was currently servicing, the department stores. Selling additional supplies might have expanded her revenue, but it would have decreased her profit and moved her from a position of dominating a market with no competition to a position that was intensely competitive.

Structuring Your Business Operation

On top of all of the advantages we have discussed so far, integrational processing also creates a structure for your business operation. It works this way:

Once you have found the heart of your business with integrational processing, you turn your point of view outward and focus on the customer you'll be serving. Once you've identified that customer, everything else is easy. Now you can communicate with that customer through targeted marketing. You can get product to that customer with a carefully designed distribution and delivery system. And because you know that customer, the product or service you produce will be something he or she will buy.

The biggest mistake people make in business is structuring their operation around their product rather than around their market. But it doesn't matter how great your product is if no one buys it. The knowledge you gain through integrational processing will let you structure your business around your customer, and your customer is simply an individualization of your market in general.

If you know how you're going to market, how you're going to distribute, and what you're going to produce, you can create an operational infrastructure that will allow you to do those three things with optimum efficiency.

The key is to keep your infrastructure as minimal as possible, and keep it focused on your market. Regardless of its size, your company needs three primary components: marketing, fulfillment services, and production. These components focus on market identification and are supported by operations.

The good news is that this is all there is to a business structure. Large or small. Corporate or individual. Public or private. That is literally it. It's marketing, fulfillment services, and production focused on the market and supported by operations.

The great fear some people have about what it takes to put a business together—where to start—ends up as nothing more than one of the by-products of integrational processing. Understand who you are and what you want. Understand how you want to extend that into the world through your business. Understand what niche you want that business to serve. And your results are immediate.

Not only have you developed a focus, provided for its internal momentum—which in business terms are called market niche and market dominance—but you have also allowed yourself to sidestep the competitive fight and developed a business structure in the process.

Do you see how integrational processing is a fundamentally useful tool to use in accomplishing a myriad of entrepreneurial tasks?

The even better news is that the business structure that looks so easy to create really is—and it's even easier and less costly to create today than it has ever been in the economic history of this country.

Let's take a moment to look back at the development of business in the United States. You'll see a very clear evolution that will help you understand not only why small business is easier today than it's ever been, but also how streamlined your business infrastructure can be.

When this country was colonized, it was, like most of the world, primarily an agricultural and small merchant society. Bartering was common and business was simple. For the next century or so, the economy of the United States revolved around the farmer, whose products were traded for necessary goods and services. During this period, the country also saw the development of a retail services industry. Goods were produced by artisans who sold their own wares. The potter ran the pottery shop. The blacksmith ran the blacksmith shop. The milliner ran the millinery shop.

Gradually we began to separate the manufacturing process from the retailing process, and a whole new industry—manufacturing—was born. In the late 1800s, the Industrial Revolution began. Factories sprang up everywhere, and smokestacks defined city skylines. The production-driven cycle of our business evolution had begun, and would continue through the early 1900s. But it was a case of the cart (businesses) pulling the horse (the market). You've heard the old joke about the early Ford automobiles—they came in any color you wanted, so long as it was black. Production drove the market. People bought what was available, and it probably didn't occur to many of them to demand anything different.

By the end of World War II, we were the most productive country in the world. Every other developing nation had been shattered by the war. While factories around the world had been burned, bombed, pillaged, and destroyed, ours were enjoying a return from war products to consumer goods. Everything from trucks to toasters was being produced in unprecedented numbers to satisfy the demands of a society eager to make up for years of sacrifice and deprivation. We didn't have to produce weapons anymore, so we took the bombs off the assembly lines and replaced them with radios and vacuum cleaners. It really didn't seem to matter what it was—people were buying it. Businesses were finding their customers not only in the United States, but around the world, as war-torn countries struggled to rebuild.

So with the infrastructure in place to produce virtually anything we wanted, production was no longer a major concern. Instead, business leaders fretted about how to get all those consumer products where they needed to be: in the hands of the buyers. So in the second half of the 1940s, the focus of our economy shifted to distribution. Still the cart was pulling the horse.

As America moved to the suburbs, regional shopping centers appeared and later developed into massive malls. Dime stores evolved into discount department stores. The corner grocery became a supermarket, which today offers customers a variety of services, including drugs, cosmetics, flowers, banking, magazines, and gifts. Multilevel marketing proved to be a massive distribution system that managed to remain very personal, and franchising became the answer to many an entrepreneur's dream while solving a distribution problem at the same time. A sophisticated interstate highway system and improved transportation technology tied everything together, both domestically and internationally.

By the early 1970s, both production and distribution were under control. So much so, in fact, that we were exporting more than just products to other countries. There was a strong market overseas for our expertise. What could we produce? Anything we wanted. What could we distribute? Anything we wanted. We were supremely confident in our abilities. Though that confidence was somewhat justified, the companies that chose to sit back, secure in their position at the top, were in for a rude awakening.

The oil embargo and resulting energy crises of 1973 sent gasoline and consumer prices soaring. At the same time, countries that had been devastated by World War II were rebounding. They had accepted our technology, built new factories, mirrored our business systems, and were busy producing quality goods. Those goods were often less expensive and more feature-rich than ours, and offered consumers an abundance of choices. Efficient international distribution systems had already been developed to tie in with our domestic distribution system. And foreign companies were able to take advantage of the structure we had built to get their products quickly and efficiently to the U.S. market.

An embarrassing number of American companies took a beating at the hands of foreign competitors before we realized that the economic focus had again shifted, this time to marketing, and before we comprehended how significant that shift was. Product differentiation had become more critical than ever. We needed to identify and meet the needs of the market.

Foreign companies couldn't beat us in production. They couldn't beat us in distribution. But they could and did beat us in marketing. They achieved success by being sensitive to the desires of the market, while we were still operating on the assumption that the market would buy whatever we produced.

We were wrong, and changes were definitely in order.

Finally, we put the horse before the cart, letting the market pull businesses in directions that would satisfy consumers. Today, production and distribution are secondary concerns for most companies. Products can be produced; they can be distributed—those are givens. The question for any business endeavor is not production and distribution, but whether or not there is a market for that product. Will someone buy it? What makes it different from competing products? And is the perception of that difference strong enough to establish a market profitable enough to be worthwhile?

Is the horse pulling the cart in your business, or vice versa?

Two New York advertising account executives definitely understood this concept a few years ago. They admittedly knew little about the beverage industry and even less about manufacturing and distribution. What they did know was that there was a market for a natural liquid refreshment without alcohol, caffeine, or artificial sugar. They found a national beverage manufacturer who could produce the product—a seltzer water—and a bottling company that would package and distribute it. From that point, all the two budding entrepreneurs had to do was concern themselves with marketing. They advertised and promoted. Orders came in, and were turned over to the manufacturer, and then to the bottler, who delivered them to the customer, who placed more orders. A simple, profitable system based on identifying the marketplace.

The marketplace is also demanding products that will protect and restore our deteriorating environment. Melvin McMahon saw a tremendous opportunity when he looked at a waste treatment plant that was using biological means. He created a bacteria specially bred to eat grease and other drain-clogging fatty waste. Bio-Care, Inc., markets these energetic little critters to restaurants, which use the system to eliminate the potentially hazardous waste products that present a constant maintenance concern to the food service industry. The success of Bio-Care comes from marketing, from the way the company communicates. Do you want to dump bacteria down your drain? Your first response is probably to think, *Of course not. There's enough bacteria down there as it is.* But would you be interested in a system that would biologically eliminate hazardous waste with no harmful effect to the environment? You'd leap at it, wouldn't you?

The successful Banana Republic clothing stores came out of identifying a market for clothing with a safari theme. In the past few years, apparel and gift items with an Australian theme have become quite popular.

These and other well-defined markets not only exist, they are abundant. The success of your own business will come when you have identified the market you want to target and learned how to effectively communicate with it.

Our market-driven economy is likely to continue through the end of this century. Certainly we must be concerned with production and distribution, but only as they support our marketing efforts. In the old days, we needed the big factories, because we were making our money on production. But times have changed. Today we can make our money on marketing.

The key point is this: if your primary focus is on identifying and communicating with a market, your operation will require a minimal infrastructure. You'll need a small office as opposed to a huge factory. You'll need fewer people. In fact, many market-driven companies are successfully operated out of a spare bedroom, building on the work-at-home trend that has mushroomed in the last few years.

Moreover, the much-publicized shift in this country to service industries provides fertile ground for small businesspeople. Service industries thrive on niche marketing. And any time your business is niche-focused, your costs are far lower, your investment minimal, and your operation downsized.

With all that aside, because the basic elements of your infrastructure are so important and are necessary to every business, we will take an in-depth look at each of them. It doesn't matter what your product or service is, or how many people you employ, or where you are located. What matters is that this structure we just crafted be in place for you to build on.

Chapter Four Highlights

—Integrational processing provides you with six business basics: focus, momentum, market niche, market dominance, the elimination of competition, and the ability to structure your business operation.

—The economy of the United States has experienced several evolutions, from agriculture and small merchant to industrial (product-driven) to distribution to market-driven.

—We are currently in a market-driven economy, which is likely to continue into the twenty-first century.

—We must put the horse before the cart and build our businesses around the demands of the marketplace.

CHAPTER FIVE

Downsizing

The Strength Behind Successful Small Business

"It is not size that counts in business. Some companies with $500,000 capital net more profits than other companies with $5,000,000. Size is a handicap unless efficiency goes with it."

—Herbert H. Casson

BEFORE WE TALK about your business system, let's take a look at downsizing. In our context, downsizing doesn't have anything to do with corporate cutbacks and layoffs. What downsizing does is allow you to stay focused on your mission statement without getting sidetracked by your infrastructure. And to operate a business any other way in the nineties definitely stacks the deck against you.

You've been hearing phrases like "lean and mean" and "trim the fat" in the business media for more than a decade. The rhetoric may be boring, but the principle is sound. You don't need to create a large infrastructure to be profitable. Quite the contrary: a large infrastructure will only get in your way.

In the case of your business system, bigger is *not* better, it's just inefficient.

As you design your infrastructure—and we'll discuss the process of doing that in detail over the next five chapters—keep this in mind: whatever it is, make sure it's absolutely essential before you spend money on it. If you can function efficiently working on the kitchen table with a typewriter and a hand-held calculator, don't buy a huge mahogany desk and credenza set along with the latest computer and laser printer.

What Does Your Market Want?

In business today, market is everything. If the market isn't either demanding it now or about to in the near future, don't do it. For example, do you need to rent an office? Unless you're in a retail operation where having a storefront is required, there's an excellent chance you don't. And starting your business at home gives you an economical way to get your company up and running before you quit your full-time job.

The Open University has taught thousands of people how to generate six-figure—and higher—incomes working from a spare room in their homes. They market with direct mail and other advertising pieces that are professionally designed and produced. They visit clients; clients don't come to them. So it makes sense that clients don't know or care whether these entrepreneurs are located in plush downtown office towers, suburban office parks, or a spare rooms in their homes.

There is a virtually limitless number of businesses that don't require commercial or retail space to be successful and profitable. The only piece of equipment Melissa bought when she started her business was a cellular phone. When she shared her story at one of my seminars, Melissa explained that when she was working as an executive secretary, it was difficult to find someone to run personal errands for her busy boss. There were plenty of package delivery services in town, but none that would send a courier into the grocery store to pick up a few items, to the dry cleaner to pick up laundry, or to a specialty shop for a gift. In short, executives who needed a professional to help out in their personal lives had nowhere to turn.

So Melissa started the Executive Gopher, an executive errand-running service. Her logo is a gopher in a business suit donning a pair of running shoes. Her infrastructure is minimal. It consists of her car, which she already owned, and a mobile phone. Her target market is busy executives who do not have someone in their lives to run miscellaneous personal errands. She doesn't need an office, her overhead is nominal, and her profits are high.

Perhaps, even though you know clients are not likely ever to want to come to see you, you still feel that you need a separate business address. Fine. Rent a post office box. Or consider taking advantage of companies like Mail Boxes Etc., whose franchises have sprung up all over the country. These facilities are usually located in strip shopping centers and provide you with an address that includes a suite number for mail and package delivery. They have a fax and copy machine for your use on a pay-as-you-go basis, and other services, including typing, notary, voice mail, office supplies, printing, and so on.

If you are going to work from home, here are a few tips:

- Create a clearly established work area. Ideally, dedicate at least one room exclusively to your business. This is essential both for tax purposes and for productivity. If you're going to deduct a portion of your home rent or mortgage as a business expense, you can't have your office doubling as a guest room. Make it a working environment, so you know that when you step into that room, you are "at work."
- Install a business telephone line. This allows you to separate business calls from personal ones. The company phone should be off-limits to family members who are not active in the business. That way you can be assured your phone is always answered in a knowledgeable and professional manner. When you are not in the office, turn on an answering machine or call-forward the line to a voice mailbox—again, with a professional message.
- Set office hours and stick to them. This applies whether your business is a part-time or full-time venture. Many people are attracted to the idea of working from home because of what they view as the flexibility it offers. But one of the biggest pitfalls of a home-based office is the multitude of distractions in the form of household tasks and demands from youngsters. Treat the yard and the laundry as though you were heading out to an office each day— those chores will be there later. Let the kids know you are not to be disturbed unless there is an emergency. Of course, if you want to build time with your family into your schedule, that's okay. It's the unscheduled interruptions that cause problems.

  Another pitfall of a home-based business is not knowing when to quit. Balance in life is essential, so set a time to turn off the light, close the door to your office, and enjoy some recreation.

- Check on zoning before you start. Before setting up a home-based business, you should check to make sure you're not violating any zoning regulations. In most communities, the understandable concern is about safety and maintaining the quality of the neighborhood. You might encounter objections if your business is in any way hazardous, will create excessive traffic, or if you want to display large signs on your home. Otherwise, you shouldn't have any problems.

If you absolutely can't work at home, either because there's no room, or because the business you've chosen requires a commercial setting, you still may not need a full office of your own. For example, is a full-time receptionist essential, or could you be just as effective sharing those services with other businesses? If you only need a conference room for a few hours each week, do you need to pay rent on it for the entire month? An executive suite situation, where you have your own office but share support services with other tenants, may be the most appropriate solution for you. Check under "Office and Desk Space Rental Service" in the yellow pages of your telephone directory for a listing of the facilities in your community.

Of course, some companies do require an office. If you're in this category, look for office space that meets your needs without a lot of expensive and unnecessary frills. Karl, one of my clients, asked me a few years ago to negotiate a lease on new office space for his advertising agency. It would have been a simple matter to contact the building's agent, drive the price down by a dollar or two per square foot, gain a few concessions, and present my client with an attractive lease. But I believe my role as a corporate attorney and advisor goes further than that. I knew the rent on his current space was extremely reasonable. The new office was considerably larger, plusher, and priced at nearly four times what he was paying. So I asked Karl why he wanted to move.

His response was that the agency was doing so well he thought it was time to relocate to more prestigious quarters. But did he need more room? No. Was there anything wrong with the offices he now occupied? No. Was he planning to make changes in his marketing, distribution, or production methods that would require the new office space? No. Would the new space improve the product he was offering his clients? Of course not.

Did I talk him out of making the move? You bet I did.

An office is only one kind of commercial space. Maybe instead of a service, your business involves a product that needs to be shipped. But that doesn't necessarily mean you should rent a warehouse.

At The Open University, we ship a tremendous amount of educational material. For the first couple of years we were in business, we did that without a warehouse. Our vendors handled it for us. We just told them what should be shipped where, and they did it and billed us accordingly. Today, our volume is high enough and consistent enough to justify handling the process ourselves. But in the early days, when there were no shipments, there was no cost—easy and efficient.

If an arrangement with vendors isn't feasible for you, then just as with your office, your first choice should be to locate at home. Is your product small enough to be stored in your garage? Ron, a former acquaintance of mine, sells the little braille plates that are attached next to the regular numbers in elevators and are required in government buildings and provided as a courtesy in others. He works strictly from his home. He runs ads in construction journals, takes orders by mail and phone, has the plates stamped out at a local machine shop, then brings them back to his garage, where he packages them for shipment.

Believe me, United Parcel Service doesn't mind picking up from residences. They're quite happy to take business wherever they can get it. And if it isn't practical to have UPS picking up and delivering at your home, either because of your own schedule or local community standards, toss the packages in your car and take them down to the UPS office. You can also arrange to have them hold anything that has been shipped to you until you can get down to pick it up yourself.

If it's not practical to work from your garage, either because you don't have one or because of your product, you still have alternatives to a traditional warehouse. You might be able to use a self-serve storage facility, or even a public warehouse that will handle shipping and receiving for you. Check in the telephone directory under warehouses to find out more about the different services that are available and their costs.

Entrepreneurial Opportunities

Downsizing offers a twofold benefit. The first, as we've discussed, is that your overhead is kept to a minimum, which increases your profits. The second is that as companies look for more efficient ways to accomplish specific functions, more business opportunities than ever are being created—and the majority of these can be operated from home.

Do you need to hire a secretary to send out an average of two letters a week? Of course not. Use a word processing service. Do you have a personal computer, a high-quality printer, and the desire to be in business for yourself? Start a word processing service.

The computer market is another good example. Most companies can operate comfortably with desktop computers rather than a huge mainframe system, and they don't need a full-time specialist to make sure their minicomputers stay up and running. When they need someone, they call in a consultant and pay only for the services they use. The recognition of that shift in the market led Pete Giarrusso to leave his corporate position as a data processing manager for free-lance consulting and ultimately his own retail computer operation, CDS Computers, a company I mentioned earlier.

Manage Your Business, Not Your Infrastructure

The whole point behind downsizing is to run your business, not your infrastructure. When you run your business, you're managing activities that will make money. When you run your infrastructure, you're spending money that offers no return.

A young woman I knew—not one of my clients—wanted to start a company that would produce newsletters for other businesses. She invested almost a year doing things like setting up her corporation, designing her logo, planning ad campaigns, looking for office space, glamorizing her portfolio, and so on. She never got around to establishing a market, acquiring clients, or producing any newsletters. She was running her infrastructure, not her business.

The application of downsizing is not limited to the start-up phase of your company. It will be a critical aspect of your operations forever. And it's easy to lose sight of the value of keeping things as streamlined as possible when profits are rolling in and you can afford those un- necessary extras. Karl's ad agency was making enough money to pay the higher rent in the fancier office, but if he lost a major client and revenues dropped for a few months, he might have found himself operating at a loss until the business was replaced.

All of the so-called "corporate downsizings" that are written about in business publications today should never have happened. If those companies had stayed lean to begin with, their infrastructures would never have become so demanding and expensive.

It's tempting to rent that nice office, even if you don't really need it. But along with the office comes carpet, window coverings, furniture, and clever decorator items that need to be purchased and maintained. Suddenly you're spending more time supervising the janitor and talking to the building manager about how the lobby is maintained than you are dealing with the marketing, fulfillment services, and production aspects of your business.

Integrational processing provides you with the tools you need to create a successful business based on who you are and what you want to do with your life. Use downsizing as a way to keep from getting bogged down with details and chores that will not move you toward your vision.

Remember, your infrastructure has three legs: marketing, fulfillment services, and production. You already know who your customer is, so begin building the first part of your business operation by com- municating effectively with that customer through marketing.

Chapter Five Highlights

—Bigger is not necessarily better; small businesses have the potential for large profits.

—Don't waste money on unnecessary infrastructure items. If you can operate your business from your home, don't rent an office.

—If you elect to work from home, respect your business as a business.

—Downsizing has resulted in the creation of more entrepreneurial opportunities.

—Pay constant attention to the operating components of your business to keep them streamlined.

CHAPTER SIX

Marketing
What Makes You Different?

"Your market has a free choice, and only by supplying what the market wants, and not by your efforts to impose your merchandise, will you get your maximum share of the market's potential."

—Walter H. Lowy

BEHIND EVERY SUCCESSFUL BUSINESS is a personality—one person projecting his or her image to the outside world. The personality behind Federal Express is Fred Smith. At Chrysler, it's Lee Iacocca. At Microsoft Corp., it's Bill Gates. Certainly these companies have a structure. They have all the required operating components. But they also have a unique collection of characteristics that reflect the driving force behind the company.

Just as Wal-Mart projects the values and attitudes of the late Sam Walton, your business projects you to the world. Your business is your alter ego, an extension of who you are, and it doesn't matter if the geography of your market extends to your neighborhood, your region, the country, or the entire world.

Remember how students are taught to fence? Marketing is a lot like that. First you create your business, which is an extension of yourself (the foil). Then you create a razor-sharp marketing strategy, so sharp that you'll be able to hit the center of your market every single time (your skill with the foil). Your market is that moving tennis ball. When you have practiced enough that you can lunge and hit that ball every time, you're ready to go into business.

You've heard of the difference between a shotgun and a rifle—I suggest you take your approach to marketing one step further. ODon't use a shotgun. Don't even use a rifle. It's not the spray of the buckshot or the speed of the bullet that counts. What counts is accuracy—use a very precise fencing foil. Because you have identified your market with integrational processing, you'll have no trouble finding and hitting it—every time.

You've already learned that each part of your organizational structure is related to your market niche, and your customer base is reflected in your operating components. The operating components of your business are marketing, fulfillment services, and production. They are all supported by operations, and they are structured in a way that will allow you to best serve your customers. You begin serving your customers by communicating with them, and the total process of that communication is called marketing.

Marketing, as you will see, is nothing more than three things: identifying your market niche, learning how to communicate with it, and then maintaining it with effective sales and customer service.

Analyze the Market

Just as your integrational processing exercises did, your market research must include two fundamental considerations: current reality and vision. You don't need a crystal ball to make reasonably accurate predictions, but you do need an understanding of the market today as it relates to both consumers and other companies. That knowledge will provide you with the ability to look into the future in order to position yourself. So where do you look today to learn what you must know about your market as it currently exists and as it can be expected to change?

Trade Publications

Your first source of information is trade journals. Read a few copies of every journal for your particular industry, and subscribe to the flagship publication. For example, in the restaurant industry, the flagship is *Nation's Restaurant News,* but you might also want to take a look at *Restaurants USA, Restaurants & Institutions, Foodservice Product News, Bartender Magazine,* or *Restaurant Business.*

In the sporting goods industry, the flagship is *The Sporting Goods Dealer,* but other publications include *Sporting Goods Business, Sports, Inc., The Sports Business Weekly,* and a variety of magazines directed to specific activities.

Trade journals are the "gossip sheets" of a particular industry—and, in this case, I don't use the term gossip in a derogatory sense. These publications are generally not flashy, but they tell you who is doing what, when and where, and the information is usually reliable.

Finding these journals requires nothing more than a trip to the library. Both the *Readers' Guide to Periodical Literature* and the *Gale Directory of Publications and Broadcast Media* provide a subject matter index and information on each publication. After you have a list of relevant trade journals, check the details, including where and when they are published, paid and nonpaid circulation, subscription and advertising rates, and who the target market is.

If your library doesn't have the information you are seeking, try contacting the Conference Board, a nonprofit, nonpartisan business network offering a variety of information services. They are located at 845 Third Ave., New York, NY 10022, and their telephone number is (212) 759-0900.

Most trade journals are not available on newsstands, and your library isn't likely to subscribe to limited circulation publications that are extremely industry-specific, so your next step is to contact the publisher for a few sample copies. The publication directories list the address and telephone number of the magazines, and a phone call should easily get you the current and one or two back issues, along with subscription information. Many of these journals are free to the trade after you complete a brief questionnaire about your business. If the one you want is not a free publication, the sample copies will help you decide if subscribing is a worthwhile investment.

Trade journals may not give you a great insight into the future, but they do give you a reasonably clear snapshot of the present.

Trade Shows, Conventions, and Conferences

Other sources for current information are trade shows and conventions. Nothing equals a trade show for convenient, concentrated exposure to the major players in any given industry. Along with informative displays on the exhibit floor, you can take advantage of workshops and seminars on a variety of related topics. Most industries have at least one or two national shows each year, along with several regional exhibitions. It's worth the investment to travel to one of the national shows. And you needn't limit yourself to the United States. If your product lends itself to exporting, you'll want to consider attending the appropriate international shows.

At the show, stop by every booth that is in any way related to your business, examine the display, and pick up literature. Somebody will be passing out plastic bags; get one and fill it up with information. Talk with the exhibitors. You'll pick up lots of ideas, identify some potential suppliers, understand more about your competition, and maybe even find a prospective customer or two.

Exhibitors have their latest and best products on display at trade shows, as well as their most recent catalogs. You'll get a preview of what you can expect to see on the market over the next few months, and you'll probably learn about what's in the long-term planning stages at specific companies.

Attending a trade show is like placing a frame around the present state of a given industry. A trade show gives you the opportunity to see just about all of the players in your industry on the playing field at one time. You'll see the biggest and the smallest. You'll see all different segments—manufacturers, wholesalers, retailers, catalogers, jobbers—as well as the businesses that provide service and support to the industry. You can chat with key people on the trade show floor. You can schmooze in the hospitality suites. You can walk up to the biggest, strongest, toughest player on the field without worrying about being stepped on, because he's at the show to talk to people. He wants to see and be seen.

You can also talk to representatives of companies very similar to your own. A gift shop in Portland, for example, isn't going to worry about competition from a gift shop in Indianapolis, so the rep or owner may not mind discussing the business in general or even what does or doesn't work specifically.

Conventions offer similar opportunities and are often tied in with trade shows. Details on conventions and shows are usually outlined in trade journals. Many industry publications list related events for the benefit of their subscribers. For example, the calendar section in just one issue of *Office Systems* included details on trade shows hosted by the National Office Machine Dealers Association and Recognition Technologies Users Association. It also listed conferences on such topics as optical information systems, as well as the dates for the National Postal Forum.

Another source is *Successful Meetings Magazine* in New York, publishers of the annual *Trade Shows & Exhibits Schedule,* which may be available at your library or local convention and visitors bureau. The price of this directory is about $85, a little steep for onetime use, but it can be ordered by calling (800) 253-6708. Or check the *National Directory of Associations,* also at the library. Professional associations often sponsor shows at national, regional, and local levels, and can give you information about what you might expect at various events. Of course, if you are serious about becoming a part of an industry, consider membership in the appropriate professional organization.

One trade show or convention is worth a thousand pages of theory about a given industry. Trade shows usually last from one to three days, and there is no other way you can see so much in such a short time while you also collect the supporting documentation.

General Publications

In addition to industry-specific information, you need related information. Learning about the industry lets you see the current reality; related information gives you a window into the future by identifying trends. So after you've read the trade journals and gone to the shows, take a look at general news publications like *Time, Newsweek,* and *Esquire.* Magazines such as these tell you more than what's happening, they tell you *why* it's happening, and they analyze the impact of current trends on the future.

If you had read *Sporting Goods Dealer* in 1975, you would have seen a few brief columns that said athletic footwear sales were likely to be up that year. What was really happening was a physical fitness revolution. People were becoming more and more health conscious, and increasing their level of participation in activities such as jogging and other forms of aerobic exercise. It was this trend that allowed Nike to move from a small, regional company to a position of leadership in the athletic footwear industry. And it was this trend that was profiled in *Esquire* in the same year. The difference is that the trade journal told you *what* was happening; the general magazine told you *why.*

In recent years none of the restaurant trade publications had given much ink to the sudden popularity of comedy clubs that began in the late 1980s. If you were, or wanted to be, in the restaurant business, that might have been relevant information for you, but you wouldn't have seen it in any trade journals. What you could have seen was an article in *Esquire* examining the trend of cable comedy specials, the skyrocketing number of comedy club franchises, and the importance of comedy in today's dining and entertainment industry.

Related articles not only offer you a window to the future, they analyze why that window is there and what you can do about it.

Customer Profile

Another source of information for current market analysis is a customer profile. Of all of the data available to you, this is by far the most significant, and yet it is the most often overlooked. The value of a customer profile applies whether you are currently in business or still in the planning stages. The most important thing you need to understand about your customers is their buying motive. Why is that individual your customer, or why will he or she be your customer?

It also helps to know other details about your customers: where they live; how much money they earn; what age groups they are in; the size of their households; the size of their businesses; how often they are likely to purchase your product; if they consider your product a luxury or a necessity.

If you are in business, take a look at the demographics of your existing customer base. If you are preparing to start a business, the best way to develop a customer profile is to model one based on the customers of the other players on your field. This means you have to find out who those customers are. How? There are three primary ways.

Observation. When my father and I first got into the sporting goods business in 1971, I didn't know a clay pigeon from a duck decoy. I knew nothing about sporting goods, and even less about who bought what and why. To learn, I took a folding chair and settled in across the street from Denmark's, the oldest, largest sporting goods store in town. That store was a virtual institution in Orlando. Its founder, Pete Denmark, had a local television show on fishing; everybody knew him, and he knew everybody. In terms of competition, he was formidable. That's why I needed to know as much about his operation and customers as possible. I needed to find out what portion of the market he *wasn't* serving so I could slide in and carve my own niche.

So I sat outside that store for days, and I cataloged everyone who walked in and walked out. If I could see what product they bought, I made a note of that. I guessed at their ages and made notes of any visible characteristics that would help distinguish them in the marketplace. It was critical to the success of my own business that I learn as much as possible about the sporting goods market in my community. Since I couldn't do it in my mind, I did it by looking.

Interviewing. Another way to get accurate information for your customer profile is with interviews. Identify at least six actual or potential customers and conduct a brief interview about what they consider important about your business.

When Chris, Kathy, and I were developing Softlab, we used the interview technique to find holes in Wang Computer's marketplace. Chris was an expert on Wang equipment, so we polled people to find out who had Wang computers, who was doing the servicing, and what the quality of that service was.

An interior designer who attended one of my seminars worked predominantly with private residences and wanted to expand into merchandising model homes. I suggested she call some of the builders she knew through events sponsored by professional organizations like the area Home Builders Association, and if possible call on the familiarity of mutual friends or associates to open a conversation. She was to call only builders who were using other interior designers, and request just a few minutes of their time on the telephone.

Her questions were to be along the lines of the following: What is your designer doing that you like the most? If you had to identify the strongest characteristic of your designer, what would it be? If you had to identify your designer's weaknesses, what would they be? If you were to make one or two recommendations as to how your designer could improve his or her operation, what would they be?

In less than five minutes on the phone, she was able to obtain more accurate information than all the speculation in the world could have provided.

The value of an interview cannot in any way be minimized. If you want an answer, ask a question. And there is no better way to ask questions than by going directly to the source, which is a customer being serviced by someone else.

There is sales potential here, too. Certainly you should not attempt to sell on your initial interview, but later, after you are up and running, call back. Remind the interviewees of your conversation, thank them again for their time and input, and let them know you have taken their suggestions to heart and designed a product or service that will meet their needs. You're off and running—not only with plenty of prospective customers, but with a product that has been developed around the feedback you have accessed from a profile of qualified customers.

Contacting Suppliers. The third and final way to complete a customer profile is to look to suppliers. Every industry has suppliers, and an excellent way to get information for your customer profile is to talk to them directly. The interior designer could take a furniture factory rep to lunch and, through a series of casual questions, find out who is ordering what. A representative of a trucking company might tell you how much product is being shipped by the other players in your industry. In the legal industry, court reporters go from office to office recording and transcribing information. Attorneys have been known to discreetly entertain people in the court-reporting business to find out who is handling cases related to their particular specialties.

In his book *Swim with the Sharks Without Being Eaten Alive,* Harvey Mackay put it very succinctly: "Knowing something about your customer is just as important as knowing everything about your product."

Without a customer profile, you cannot expect to consistently reach and expand your market—and you won't be in business for long.

Time Warps

Depending on your type of business and geographic location, an interesting phenomenon I call time warps may be considered as part of your market research.

There are particular areas of the country or world that are by nature the trendsetters. They stay a few steps ahead of everyone else in what they do. For fashion, it's Rome. What's fashionable in Rome today will probably be fashionable in the United States two years from now. It's a time warp. What I saw in Rome's clothing stores in 1985, I didn't see in New York until 1987.

Paris leads the world in retailing concepts. When I visited Paris in 1972, I saw retailing techniques that were not incorporated into stores in the United States until 1974 to 1976.

Japan sets the trends in electronic gadgetry.

As to the food industry, what you see being eaten in California today is likely to be popular in New York a year from now, in Florida two years from now, and in the Midwest a few years after that. Californians were eating health foods long before the rest of the nation got into the act—something that General Mills Restaurants obviously didn't consider with the Good Earth Restaurants. (I'll tell you the full story of this chain in Chapter Eight.)

California also sets trends in the legal arena. Homeowners began suing their community associations in that state first; the idea made its way to Florida and is now spreading out among condominium and homeowners associations across the country.

The point is, you can use time warps by letting what is happening in a particular part of the world today tell you what will be happening in your part of the world tomorrow.

Other sources for market information include the business department at a nearby university, the Small Business Administration, the Census Bureau, chambers of commerce, bankers, the annual reports of public companies, and government agencies that regulate specific industries. *Findex: Directory of Market Research Reports, Studies and Surveys* from the Cambridge Information Group in Gaithersburg, Maryland, lists eleven thousand consumer, market, and industry studies. The price of the directory is approximately $340; call (800) 843-7751 for additional information. You can probably come up with a few more sources I haven't thought about—I hope you do.

BEST PLACES TO LOCATE MARKET INFORMATION

Your marketing strategy begins with a thorough understanding of your market as it exists today and what the forecasts are for the future. The best places you can find this information are:

Trade publications	Conventions
General interest news and business publications	Conferences
	Customer profiles
Trade shows	Time warps

Develop Your Marketing Message

The first part of effective marketing is understanding who your customer is and why he or she buys from you, and then developing a product consistent with that information. The second part of marketing involves developing your marketing message.

A marketing message is basic, simple, and has just three parts: who you are, what makes you different, and how the customer can participate. Of course, you must tell people who you are, and most companies—big or small—will do that. But that alone is not sufficient. You must also tell people what distinguishes you from other companies and how they can buy from you.

A consistent characteristic of strong marketing organizations is that they never miss an opportunity to broadcast their marketing message. In every ad for Banana Republic, you'll be reminded of their natural fabric, safari-themed clothing and where the nearest store is. In every Sharper Image catalog and retail store, the theme is also clear: these are high-tech products that are difficult to obtain anywhere else, but you can buy them by calling a toll-free number and having your credit card ready.

The Difference Is

What makes you different is, of course, the market niche you've created for yourself. You have found your place on the playing field; you should remind people of it all the time. If you're on the five-yard line, tell them you're the company on the five-yard line, and do it so consistently that when they think of the five-yard line, they automatically think of you.

When you established your business identification and market niche, you determined what would make you different so you could eliminate the competition. Now you need to explain that difference in a way that will provide prospective customers with recognizable benefits.

Here are some things that might make your company different:

Location. You could be the only company in the area that does what you do, such as the Westside Cleaners or Downtown Office Supply. Or your location could have some other significance, like "easy access," or "near a major intersection," or even "off the beaten path, but worth the trip."

Format. Present your business just a little bit differently from the way other similar companies present themselves. Instead of inviting customers to browse through your store or showroom, install them in a private viewing area and bring merchandise to them. Preparing food at the table in view of the diners has been a popular format for many restaurants. The format of Fotomat—drive-up film developing—quickly distinguished that company from every other place that processed film.

Service. You can distinguish yourself with service by personally greeting customers when they walk into your facility, by following up after the sale to make sure the product is operating satisfactorily, by guaranteeing emergency response within a designated period of time, or by offering any type of service your competitors don't. But remember that saying you offer good service is a cliché; don't promote it unless you're prepared to provide it.

Cleanliness. One of the things that sets fast-food restaurants like McDonald's apart is that you can pretty much count on the cleanliness of each restaurant, no matter where you are. Grocery stores also use cleanliness as a selling point. Modern gyms and spas like Bally Health Clubs capitalize on their reputations for sanitary facilities. Even automobile service facilities are finding this is a significant drawing factor.

Quality. During the eighties, we were bombarded with advertising messages about quality, and it's possible the public has become just a little jaded on this topic. Like service, talking about quality can also be clichéd. But if you experience fewer complaints and service calls because you do things right the first time, play that up as something that makes you different. Remember that quality usually means higher price. To promote the highest quality goods at the cheapest price is inconsistent and will confuse the public, because it doesn't make sense. If you're selling quality, price accordingly.

Customer Support. Particularly as we add more and more high-tech items to our homes and offices, customer support becomes increasingly critical. For example, most computer software companies have customer support departments with dedicated telephone lines to answer questions from users. But this difference isn't limited to high-tech products; home and garden stores are just one of an assortment of retail and business-to-business operations that often have resident "experts" to give advice and answer questions.

Personal Service. This is often where the smaller company sets itself apart from the giant. It's the independent bank where customers are greeted by name. It's the clothing store that keeps personal information about you on file, and calls you to remind you of your wife's birthday or tell you a special sale is coming up. It's the office supply store whose sales rep calls periodically to see if you need supplies. It's anything you do to make each customer feel that he or she is more than just a source of revenue to you. The florist I use, House of Flowers in Orlando, sends me a list each month of everyone I sent flowers to during that month last year, with a note asking me if I want to send flowers again. It's a great way to remind me of birthdays and anniversaries. It's also an excellent sales tool, and a wonderful example of personal service.

Convenience. People generally prefer to buy from companies that make it easy for customers to do business with them. The proliferation of convenience stores, such as 7–11 and Circle K, is the most visible example of the buying public's preference on this score. But there are other ways you can offer convenience to your customers, such as a streamlined ordering process, drive-through windows, or merchandise displayed in a manner that makes things easy to find. With convenience, as with quality, comes additional price. You expect to pay more for groceries purchased at a convenience store than for those from a regular supermarket, because the convenience has value attached to it.

Delivery System. Is there anything special about the way you get your product to your customer? You may buy Domino's Pizza for the taste, but chances are what you're really buying is the speed and convenience of their delivery system. A variety of personal and professional services—from veterinary care to bicycle repair to bookkeeping—are setting up mobile operations, differentiating themselves by going to their customer, rather than having their customer come to them.

Knowledge. If you're an expert in your field, position yourself as such. Frequently the fees you pay to doctors, attorneys, and accountants are based more on what they know than what they actually do. You've heard the story of the plumber who comes in, looks over the broken sink, twists one screw, and says, "That will be fifty dollars." The customer asks, "It costs fifty dollars to twist one screw?" "No," the plumber replies, "it doesn't cost anything to twist the screw; it costs fifty dollars to know which screw to twist."

Uniqueness. If you have a true one-of-a-kind operation, play it up. Pier One Imports carries a line of unique gift and decorator items. Kids At Large, a company that manufactures and markets clothes for overweight children, doesn't have any competition.

Speed. The demand for instant gratification has never been stronger. Fast food is an obvious example, but even sit-down restaurants are adding menu items guaranteed to be served in ten minutes. Lots of photo shops promise one-hour film processing. A few years ago, Eckerd Drugs built a major ad campaign around their fast service "because America won't wait."

Inventory. Offering customers a wide selection of products, or being able to assure them you'll never be out of stock on certain items, or having the accessories on hand that go with a major purchase are all ways inventory can make you different. Sometimes what makes you different is inventory narrowness, like Athletic Attic or Size 5-7-9 Shops. Sometimes it's inventory breadth; the motto of Behr's Shoe Center in downtown Orlando is "We can fit any human."

Price. Price only counts as a difference when you are charging less than your competition. Discount stores like K mart and Wal-Mart capitalize on price very effectively. Neiman Marcus does not.

Let me digress for a moment. I'd like to make an extra comment about price: price is never to be used as a distinguishing difference in your marketing message unless it is your primary difference. If you have structured your company around a discount operation, use price as a differentiating characteristic. But if you're not a discount operation, don't use price; if you do, you'll create expectations that are not consistent with what you will be delivering.

The airline industry offers us some excellent examples of how *not* to use price as a difference. Some quality full-service carriers have resisted the temptation provided by deregulation to offer a large number of seats at deeply discounted fares. They have built a loyal customer base on timely operations, well-maintained aircraft, and personnel who are knowledgeable and professional. The true discount carriers make no pretenses about what they are. You definitely won't get a meal and may not even get a drink, the seats are small, there are absolutely no comfort-related amenities, and if they provide baggage check service, you'd probably be wise not to use it. You're getting the best price, and, if that's what you want, you'll put up with the rest.

The airlines that got into trouble were full-service operations that began hawking price as a distinguishing characteristic to gain a larger market share. But when you use price in this way, you're basing all customer loyalty on that low price. When the rates go up, you lose your market share. Basic economics will tell you that a full-service operation cannot make a profit collecting only discount prices, no matter what the industry. A number of full-service airlines selling below-cost fares either lost so much money they were forced into bankruptcy, or they eventually had to raise prices to cover operating costs and lost so much of their market share they were forced into bankruptcy anyway. Either way, the results were the same.

A custom residential builder might tag his promotional pieces with "Quality homes for the discriminating buyer, priced from $500,000." That certainly tells you who his target market is, and you can bet he doesn't spend his time talking with middle-income first-time home buyers. And perhaps you've noticed that Chevrolet offers rebates on its cars, but Rolls-Royce doesn't. Which one uses price as a differentiating factor?

Luxury department stores may include prices in some of their ads and even promote special sales, but price is not a fundamental part of their marketing message. Discount department stores, on the other hand, are constantly badgering you with claims of low prices. You probably shop in both types of stores. There are certain items you buy wherever you can get the best price. For other products, you are more concerned with such considerations as quality merchandise and personal service. In the first case, you probably don't care if you're in a K Mart or a Wal-Mart. In the second case, it's likely you have developed a strong sense of loyalty to the specialty shop where a customer service representative maintains a file of personal information such as your birthday and anniversary dates, sizes, and color preferences.

Of course, even K Mart and Wal-Mart don't sell exclusively on price. K Mart also promotes their designer labels; Wal-Mart brags about products made in America.

The point is, you may be able to buy your customers with price, but remember that they won't stay bought when the prices go up.

There's nothing wrong with an off-price structure if it is indeed consistent with the perception and perceived benefit of the operation. If you're offering name-brand pool supplies at a lower price than anyone else in town because you're buying in quantity and passing along the savings to your customers, that's fine. But would you go to a brain surgeon who offered volume discounts? Would you jump out of an airplane wearing a parachute from a cut-rate packer?

The bottom line on price is this: if you make it part of your marketing message, it will be both a primary and permanent part of your public image. Before making price your difference, be absolutely certain that's what you want to do.

Product. For some companies, the product itself is what makes the difference. Custom designed and manufactured items fall in this category.

Add-On Benefits. If you take an ordinary item and do something to make it different, it's an add-on benefit. Most malls have at least one store like Monograms Plus or Emblems Plus where the merchandise is average, but the attraction is the personalizing of the items with a monogram or other message. A key chain is a key chain, but add your initials at Things Remembered and it becomes something special.

Image. When your product is desirable because it has your name on it, your difference is image. Companies like Gucci, Rolex, and Neiman Marcus understand this and promote a sense of elitism among their customers.

Regardless of what the difference is, understand that difference is everything. Create a difference and you've got a business. Without a difference, there is no business. And never lose an opportunity to make that difference part of your marketing message.

How Can I Participate?

The final part of your marketing message, letting prospective customers know how he or she can participate in what you have to offer, is so obvious that it often gets overlooked. Even longtime promotion professionals have been known to get so wrapped up communicating the difference that they forget to tell people how to take advantage of it. Have you ever seen an ad that said, "Call us today for more information," but didn't have a telephone number in it? You must let people know how they can participate, whether it's by calling, coming in, sending in a coupon, or whatever is appropriate for your business.

Once you have put together these three essential components of your marketing message—who you are, what makes you different, and how your customer can participate—it's time to disseminate that message to your market niche.

Communicating with the Marketplace

Communicating with your market is simply the delivery of your marketing message, and there's an effective and an ineffective way to do that. There are a number of methods you can use to communicate with your marketplace. They are primarily advertising, public relations, and reciprocal communications. Let's take a look at each of these, and how you can best use them.

Advertising

There is an abundance of articles, books, and courses on the mechanics of advertising, covering how to write copy, how to design layouts, which medium to select, and so on. But the purpose of this book is not to teach you the technique of creating advertising copy, but rather to cut through all of the misinformation about advertising so you can deal specifically with what is essential and what works.

Regardless of which medium you select to carry your marketing message, there are two major categories of advertising: institutional and direct response.

Institutional Advertising. Rather than selling a product, institutional advertising does what its name implies: it promotes the institution.

The objective of this form of advertising—sometimes called corporate advertising—is not to sell a specific product, but to create a favorable image of, or attitude toward, the company sponsoring the advertising. The idea is that if you get a nice, warm feeling—or whatever the appropriate or relevant reaction is—about the company from institutional advertising, then you'll think of them when you're ready to buy. My reaction to that is: don't count on it.

Companies without goods to sell may also employ institutional advertising, as Perrier did when traces of the cancer-causing chemical benzene turned up in their product and the popular bottled water was pulled from store shelves around the world. Public utilities and other organizations dependent upon the goodwill of the general public feature institutional themes in their advertising copy. Manufacturers with strong research departments will frequently tell the public that research is their most important product. Oil companies are especially good at this. For example, you don't have a choice about which electric, water or local telephone company to use, but these companies still want you to feel good about being their customers so they'll run warm, fuzzy ads designed to let you know what a caring company they are. But for most businesses, and certainly for small businesses, institutional advertising is generally the most expensive and least effective type of advertising you can do.

There are three major problems with institutional advertising.

The first is that it's not a complete communication; it doesn't carry your full marketing message. In a Merrill Lynch commercial, the bull moves across the screen, and the message is that Merrill Lynch is bullish on America. My response is, so what? That ad does not contain any information on how the viewer can participate in Merrill Lynch. That ad, taken by itself, does not offer a complete marketing message. Now, the people who do the advertising for Merrill Lynch aren't stupid, and their television commercials are only part of a broad campaign using a variety of media. The television commercial is designed to give you a feeling of confidence and trust about Merrill Lynch so you'll respond to a print ad requesting direct action or, at the very least, not hang up on one of their brokers when they call. Nonetheless, the TV ad still isn't a full communication that tells their customers how to participate in their service.

The second problem with institutional ads is they do not produce feedback, which, in marketing, is absolutely essential. The approach says you want to talk, but don't need to listen to the response. There is no way for the market to respond to the ad, so you don't know if it was an effective campaign. You don't know how many people saw your ads or how they reacted to them. For most small and midsize businesses, the goodwill intent of institutional ads is not a worthwhile investment, especially when you get no feedback from the message.

The third problem is that without feedback you have no way of knowing whether your ad was self-supporting. You need feedback to know if you are hitting the center of your market. You also want to know in dollars and cents how much you invested in the campaign and how much money you made.

When you're asked to "buy radio spots telling everybody about your company" or to run your business card every week in the local paper, that's institutional advertising, and it will probably be worthless. You might as well take the money an ad would cost and treat yourself to a night on the town—at least that way you'll get some fun out of those dollars.

Let me make something perfectly clear: I'm not suggesting that you shouldn't advertise. What I'm saying is that you shouldn't waste your limited resources on ads that only generate goodwill. You want your ads to attract customers, and ultimately, to create additional sales and profits.

Because institutional advertising does not produce feedback, it is basically ineffective as a revenue-producing tool. It can't help you stay at the center of your marketplace because it won't tell you where your market is. And it doesn't give you any indication of whether your advertising budget is being invested well. Some people will argue that institutional advertising helps promote name recognition and goodwill. That's fine for public utilities operating in a monopoly situation or huge corporations with large budgets, but if you need a positive return on your marketing dollars, you would be wiser to choose direct response advertising.

Direct Response Advertising. Direct response advertising is also called action advertising, because it's a call to action. It's an ad that encourages a response by saying, "Here's who I am, here's what makes me different, and here's how you can participate with me right now." It's a complete communication.

Because a direct response ad tells the market how to participate, you have a way to count the people who respond. Direct response ads include a message to call, or come in, or a coupon for a discount or free sample. Coupons, by the way, make it especially easy to determine the success of a particular promotion: count the coupons, and you know how many people responded. But coupons are not essential; telephone calls can be coded with extensions or names to see who responded to which ad. A less precise measurement is comparing sales figures during the time of a special promotion against those during a control period. The point is that you have a valid way to measure the results of your campaign, so you know whether you have a winner or not.

In the early 1970s, I decided to promote the tennis department in my sporting goods store by bringing in an internationally known player to meet people and sign autographs on a Saturday morning. The promotion cost about $3,000. The normal sales volume for that store on a Saturday was $1,400. When we opened the store on Saturday morning, there were twenty-two people in the parking lot waiting to see the tennis star. We did $3,000 in sales, which meant an extra $1,600 at a 50 percent gross profit margin, giving us a contribution to overhead of $800. We spent $3,000 to produce $800—definitely not something we wanted to do again.

For our next promotion, we brought in a body builder who was just beginning to get well known in this country. We spent the same amount to promote him. When the store opened on the morning of his appearance, there were nearly a thousand people in the parking lot. And instead of selling $3,000 worth of merchandise as we had done during the tennis promotion, we sold $14,000 worth of Olympic weight sets and other physical training equipment—$12,600 in sales over our normal volume, resulting in a contribution to overhead of $6,300. Not only that, we then had a thousand people who had been in the store, seen the physical fitness department, and would probably come back when they needed something else.

The ads we ran for both of these promotions were direct response ads. They included our complete marketing message, and told people they could participate by coming to the store at a certain time on a certain day to meet a celebrity.

Twenty-two people chose to participate in the tennis promotion by coming down to meet the tennis star. This told me right away that promoting tennis by bringing in someone famous was not a wise investment of my advertising dollars. After we did the body builder promotion, which drew a thousand people, I realized that we might not want to bother with promoting tennis at all.

It was clear from these two promotions that significantly more people were interested in physical fitness and training than in tennis. And it was simply smart business to promote the aspect of the sporting goods store that was profitable.

Both promotions were structured to allow us actually to count the people who responded. What's more, they told us something very significant about the center of the marketplace.

At the time, it was "common knowledge" that if you had a sporting goods store, you had to have a wide selection of tennis products. Physical training items were almost an afterthought. But tennis sales, which had increased steadily through the late sixties, had begun to flatten out when the fitness craze was starting. Because these changes were just beginning, they were not reflected in our sales and inventory histories. With direct response advertising, we were able to quickly see that most of the people who made up our current market weren't particularly interested in tennis; they were interested in developing their bodies with exercise equipment. Now we knew where to focus our attention.

Direct response ads give you immediate feedback on your market. Sure, by tracking inventory, we would have eventually realized that the demand in sports equipment was shifting from tennis to fitness— *if* we had invested fast enough in inventory not to have lost the market. But we probably would have lost a lot of fitness equipment sales while we were waiting to analyze history. We would have trailed the market instead of leading it. So by using direct response ads, we were able to take the data produced by the those ads and increase sales.

At best, advertising is an inexact science. There is no way to accurately predict the success of any campaign in advance—you can only measure the results when it's over, and then model future campaigns after the ones that went well. And you measure by maximizing every opportunity for feedback. Direct response advertising gives you that measurability by providing a complete communication with your market and letting you know whether your promotions are self-supporting and profitable.

A final word on advertising: don't view it as an expense. It's only an expense, a necessary evil, if it's institutional. Direct response advertising is an investment in revenue production. For every dollar you put into direct response advertising, you can expect a certain number of dollars back. Your actual ratio will depend on your specific circumstances, but direct response advertising is not an expense. Electricity is an expense. Stationery is an expense. Direct response advertising is an investment in revenue production. It provides you with a vehicle to make money while you communicate with your market on a regular basis.

Remember, advertising is just one way to disseminate your marketing message to your market niche. You pay for it, so you control it. And since you control it, make sure it says something that will result in profits for your company.

ADVERTISING CHECKLIST

You should be able to answer yes to each of the following questions:

1. Is the advertisement a complete communication?

    a. Does it tell who I am?
    b. Does it tell what makes me different?
    c. Does it let prospective customers know how they can participate in my business?

2. Does the advertisement allow me to measure or count my responses?

3. Do I have a vehicle for measuring in dollars whether or not the ad was productive?

ADVERTISING ANALYSIS FORM

Cost of product_____

Sale price of product_____

Cost of promotion_____

Number of responses to promotion (calls received, coupons re-
deemed, etc.)_____

Average sales volume before marketing campaign_____

Sales volume at end of marketing campaign_____

Profit (or loss) during campaign_____

Public Relations

Another way to communicate with your market is through public relations. Direct response advertising beats institutional advertising hands down. Public relations is even more powerful than direct response advertising, although it is not necessarily geared to specific promotions.

As a small business, you won't have a public relations department, but make no mistake about this: you have public relations. They might be good, and they might be bad—but you have them. Ignore your public relations and at best you will miss some wonderful opportunities for exposure to your market; at worst your image may become so tarnished that recovery is impossible.

Public relations is important for two main reasons: it's more effective than advertising, and it's much less expensive. For example, we have invested thousands of dollars on magazine ads for the *Successful Living Library* available through The Open University. Yes, we've been making sales from those ads, but those sales were nothing compared to the volume we experienced after a writer happened to mention our videotapes in an unsolicited article in *USA Weekend.* That one piece generated more sales than all the advertising we had done combined.

Be sure you understand the difference between public relations and publicity. The former is how your company relates to the public, and the latter is the result of your efforts to gain the attention of the public. That you sponsor a children's sports team is public relations; the recognition you receive in the league program is publicity. Both are important.

Some guidelines for effective PR:

Show, Don't Tell. Your marketing message—who you are, what makes you different, and how people can participate—is an integral part as much of your public relations efforts as it is of your advertising. But though the message doesn't change, the method does. In advertising, you tell; in public relations, you *show*. In fact, the degree to which you tell in PR is the degree to which you automatically undermine your believability. Don't *tell* someone you're good at what you do; *show* them.

When I wanted to acquire new clients for my law practice, I offered a free seminar on contracts. I didn't need to tell the people who attended the seminar that I'm a good lawyer; I showed them by explaining how they could protect themselves with the right kind of contracts, and how to avoid trouble with the wrong contracts. My presentation was thorough, my handouts professionally prepared, and I was careful to communicate with my audience on a level they understood. That showed them I am a good lawyer. But if I had wound up the seminar by saying, "By the way, I want you to know I'm a really good lawyer," I would have seriously weakened my credibility.

You also don't tell people about all the good deeds you do—although good deeds are a valuable public relations vehicle. The insurance firm with a community-conscious public image never says, "We're a community-conscious company." They show that they are by doing things like donating funds to nonprofit community organizations and letting their employees take extended lunch hours one day a week to deliver Meals on Wheels. Not only will these actions speak for themselves, but other people will begin to repeat the message on your behalf. I know a local businessman who goes to great lengths to downplay his generous civic contributions. I'm not sure if he is truly modest or just very shrewd, because people all over town talk about his kindness and generosity. He doesn't have to say a word.

Be Consistent. A consistent and powerful public relations message is stronger than any amount of advertising could possibly be. Its strength lies in the fact that it is not advertising. It's not a paid message, it's a testimonial. It's people outside your company telling one another what you would like for them to know about you. So it must be consistent both in content and context.

Over the years, Exxon Corporation's public relations department worked to build an image of a caring company, but that image was destroyed almost overnight by the way the company handled the *Valdez* oil spill in Prince William Sound. The public perception—right or wrong—was that Exxon executives didn't know or truly care about the incredible ecological damage done to the Alaskan coastline.

By contrast, when Ashland Oil spilled 750,000 gallons of diesel fuel into the Monongahela and Ohio rivers in 1988, the company emerged from the disaster with a public image that was almost better than before. Why? Ashland's chairman and CEO, John Hall, went directly to the spill's site, made himself and other top executives available for any and all questions, pledged to clean up the mess, and accepted complete responsibility for the accident.

Both situations were tragic, with tremendous potential for negative consequences to the environment as well as to the corporate image and balance sheet. The difference was in consistency. Hall, by the way, was honored as "Outstanding Crisis Manager of 1988" by Carnegie-Mellon University's Graduate School of Industrial Administration.

Lack of consistency leads to misunderstanding. When people do not understand a company's position, they don't want to be customers. It's not that they'll buy sometimes and not other times—they won't buy at all, ever! They reject the person or the business or the product line because they don't understand it.

Put Yourself in Front of Your Customer. The final rule of effective public relations is that you should position yourself in front of the end user. As a businessperson also operating as an attorney, I am reluctant to invest my time on a bar association committee consisting of other lawyers who practice the same type of law I do. There may be—and have been—circumstances that give me a totally altruistic reason for sitting on a bar association committee. If that's the case, I serve on the committee, but I don't consider it part of my public relations efforts—it's simply something I do because I privately believe it's important.

If I'm on a bar association committee for public relations purposes, I make it one that will either put me in front of the public or that includes attorneys who are likely to refer clients to me. Though we politely call one another professional colleagues, in fact other attorneys are my competitors. They don't buy legal services from me—they want my clients. So for the bar association, I served on three committees: the speakers committee, where we spoke to civic organizations; the media committee, which was responsible for communicating news about our organization to the public through the media; and the mediation, or dispute settlement committee, which also brought me in contact with the public.

But even though these bar association committees provided me with some publicity, when I'm looking for positive exposure in the community, I'm much better off sitting on the board of the Heart Association or the Opera Guild, where I will routinely attend luncheons with people who make generous charitable donations. These are successful, civic-minded people whom I want as clients.

If you're in the sporting goods business, you won't find any customers by serving on the board of the National Association of Sporting Goods Dealers. You'll benefit more by directing your efforts to the YMCA, the local boys clubs, the Police Athletic League, and similar organizations. Those are the groups that buy sporting goods.

If you sell women's career clothing, you probably won't find many customers in your local merchants' association. Get involved in a couple of professional women's groups to find prospective buyers.

What you want is exposure to your relevant market, not to the colleagues and competitors within your own industry.

Getting the Publicity You Want

How do you get publicity? You can't buy time on the news, but there are a wide variety of ways you can gain that visibility.

Articles. Getting published in the magazines and newspapers your customers read is an excellent way to establish yourself as an expert in your industry. Some trade publications will even pay you while they give you a level of exposure no amount of money could buy. Chris, one of my partners in Softlab, wrote a regular column for a computer magazine. He was paid a token fee for each article, but he received so many inquiries that resulted in consulting jobs, it would have been worth it for him to pay the magazine. Contact the publications serving your target market and ask for their submission guidelines. End each article with a tag line identifying you, your company, and your location. If you're not comfortable with your own writing abilities, hire someone to ghostwrite for you. You can locate a freelancer by calling the editors of local publications and asking for referrals.

Seminars. Sponsor seminars to help your market learn to use your products more efficiently. Almost any business has the potential to offer seminars in a professional, sales, or technical capacity. A computer store might hold a half-day free session on how to maintain a computer and avoid service calls. A building supply center could offer a series of classes for the do-it-yourselfer.

Seminars give you the opportunity to show, not tell, what you are all about. When I used to teach seminars in Orlando, where my law practice is, I would always end up with twenty or thirty new clients. If someone is interested enough in your product to attend a seminar, they are likely to purchase it from you rather than from someone else after the training is over. The customer goodwill that comes from giving your market "something for nothing" is immeasurable, and will go a long way toward building customer loyalty.

Speeches. Hit the "rubber chicken circuit" by making yourself available as a speaker to every professional, fraternal, and service organization in town. Most of these groups meet weekly, and they are always looking for speakers. You won't get paid, but you will get a free meal. Sometimes it's even edible.

When I first started my law practice, I got a list of all the civic clubs in town and sent a letter to each one, telling them what my qualifications were and what I could speak on. Believe me, groups like the Lions, Rotary, Kiwanis, Optimists, Civitan, and so on, are hungry for speakers—especially ones who don't charge a fee. I would give a twenty-minute talk, answer some questions, and pass out a few business cards. Within one month after I opened my office, I was covering my overhead—in other words, I had enough income to pay for my office, my secretary, the phones. A significant number of my clients came from contacts made when I spoke.

Media Appearances. Let the public affairs coordinators at local radio and television stations know you are available for guest appearances and make some program suggestions. To get on specific talk shows, contact the program's producer.

Even though radio and television stations are no longer required to devote a certain portion of their programming to community affairs, they still do it. Cable systems have public access channels you may be able to take advantage of; legislation in this area is constantly changing, so check with your local cable operators for complete details.

If you're in the swimming pool business, offer to go on a show and talk about pool safety. If you're in the building business, you could do a program on how to choose a builder, what qualifications to look for, and what will alert the customer to a potential problem.

One of the most effective media promotions I ever did was a series a few years ago on the noon news of a local television station—the CBS affiliate in Orlando—called "Taxpayer's Alert." Once a week, I'd be on the air for five minutes discussing tax information. The viewers loved it, so the sponsors loved it, which meant the station loved it— and I expanded my own visibility, enhanced my reputation, and picked up some new clients in the bargain.

Until recently, I did two call-in talk shows—"Money Line" and "Legal Line"—alternate weeks on the noon news. I took calls and answered questions from viewers on the air. Before I could get back to my office—about a twenty-minute drive from the television station— my staff would have fielded a dozen or so calls from people who had seen me but couldn't get through on the program. A call-in television or radio program is an excellent way to generate participation from potential customers.

Media Releases. When your company does something noteworthy, issue an announcement to the media. Media releases cover new products, new clients, awards, special events, anniversaries, new staff, existing personnel who have been promoted, and more. Analyze the business section of your newspaper to determine the type of news they print and what columns or departments cover what areas, then adapt things happening within your company to suit their needs. Radio stations often have some sort of a community bulletin board and will use news about local companies in their business reports.

Once, at a trade show, I happened to overhear someone grumbling about why his competitors were always being quoted in articles and he never was. I asked if he ever sent out media releases. He said he didn't. I asked if any reporters knew who he was. He looked embarrassed and suddenly saw someone he needed to talk to. But it's a safe bet to assume that his competitors were getting mentioned and he wasn't because they had established a relationship with the media by sending out regular releases and positioning themselves as experts.

Of course, as you do this, be careful not to overload writers and editors with non-news stuff. It's also important to remember that the media is not obligated to publish anything you submit, so don't get pushy. Alienate an editor, and you might find that the only time you can get your company's name in print is if you're the subject of a criminal investigation or worse. But, for the most part, local papers want to publish news about local business, and so long as they have room, they'll probably print what you send them. Just remember you always risk having a major news event eclipse your own announcements, so don't be disappointed when certain items don't make print.

Community Relations. It is just plain good business to return some of your profits to the community where you earned them. Choose a nonprofit and noncontroversial civic organization to support. Avoid affiliating your company with religious, politically partisan, or otherwise socially sensitive groups; you can alienate large portions of your market by taking a stand on an emotional issue. If you feel strongly about a controversial issue, support it privately.

Nonprofit groups need and appreciate contributions of goods and services, which are known as in-kind donations. More to the point, this is a great opportunity to *show* people how good you are. If you are an air conditioning contractor, provide free maintenance and repair to the local homeless shelter. If you have enough employees and are located in a high-density area, sponsor a blood drive and arrange for the blood bank's mobile unit to visit your office. Encourage employees to volunteer, and support their efforts. Your involvement will *not* remain a secret.

Organizations. Establish membership in professional organizations to enhance your image. Many associations serve as a sort of Better Business Bureau for their own industries. If your memberships carry an element of prestige, be sure to indicate them on your promotional literature. Business groups, such as your local chamber of commerce, will offer you a networking vehicle.

Sponsorships. There are opportunities out there to sponsor just about anything, from bowling teams to contests to major publicity events. The key is to make the sponsorship count. If your business is silk-screening sports uniforms, sponsoring just about any type of sporting event will be a benefit. If you're an orthodontist, sponsoring a kids' team is a subtle way to put your name in front of the parents who ultimately decide which practitioner will put braces on their children's teeth. When CDS Computers sponsored a Little League team, the company sold enough computers to parents of players to earn back easily the cost of the sponsorship and still make a profit.

You might want to sponsor a wine and cheese party at your home as a fund-raiser for a worthy cause. If your target market is other businesses, contact your chamber of commerce about sponsoring one of their events. That will give you plenty of exposure with chamber members. Or you could sponsor a contest; either put it on yourself, or team up with other businesses and the local media to make a tremendous splash.

Scholarships. Award scholarships to deserving students who are studying to enter your field. You will receive publicity when you announce that you are seeking applications for the program, as well as when you announce the recipients. Scholarships don't have to be large to be sincerely appreciated, and you can set up the qualifications and terms yourself. Your scholarship program may also be a tax de-duction; check with your accountant to be sure.

Giveaways. Everybody loves to get something for nothing. Your give-aways don't have to be expensive, but they should relate in some way to your business. They should also be useful. I've seen too many companies give away some very clever items that were not cheap, but were worthless because they weren't practical. Your promotional items need to be tailored to your market just as your product line is. And whatever you're giving away, be sure to structure your program so you can measure the return on your investment in the same way you did with your direct response advertising.

A grocery store in Dallas held a truly creative giveaway a few years ago. It was near Christmas, and the store arranged for Santa Claus to fly into their parking lot on the traffic helicopter from a local radio station. The only way kids could get in to see Santa was if they brought a canned good to donate to the needy. The store matched each can of food collected.

The directors of various social services agencies were on hand to thank the youngsters and to reinforce the positive impact of their do-nations. The radio station had promoted the event for weeks. The newspaper wrote articles on it. And thousands of kids (with their parents) showed up—and most of them probably went shopping while they were there.

By staging this giveaway, the store positioned itself to be seen as a caring corporate citizen. What's more, the store provided an education tool for children to learn to be community conscious, and generated some great PR.

Newsletters. Growing in popularity, newsletters are an efficient way to communicate with your market. Like seminars, they allow you to show, not tell. Studies indicate that people are much more inclined to read a newsletter than any other piece of direct mail advertising. Keep them short, informative, and entertaining, always remembering to show not tell. KeyCom, a telephone interconnect company, produces a quarterly complimentary newsletter with the following regular features: news about any changes within the company; details on new products or services; tips on how to use the telephone more effectively; a customer profile; and a trivia contest. Customer response has been overwhelmingly positive.

At The Open University, we produce *Wealth Builder Monthly,* which offers sound business advice and fulfills a basic PR function. It communicates our marketing message and indicates our expertise to our market.

Invitationals. You can generate a lot of snob appeal with an invitational. If you have access to celebrities, arrange a party and invite people to meet them. Political figures are also good draws. You might want to organize a group to attend a major sporting event, especially if you have access to a private viewing box. Take advantage and tie into what's going on in your community. Because of Orlando's close proximity to Cape Canaveral, shuttle launches always get a lot of attention. I know one business owner who stocks his motor home with plenty of refreshments and invites key customers to drive over to the Cape with him to watch the shuttles go up. The customers love it. They have a great time even when the flight gets scrubbed at the last minute.

One final tip about public relations: don't fall into the trap of believing that publicity is "free advertising." While you don't have to pay for the media time, you *will* have to invest at least some money and time in an effective public relations program. Sometimes it's little more than the postage to mail out media releases or announce your availability as a speaker. Other times you may opt to make a civic contribution that's quite substantial. And, of course, you can't control publicity the way you can advertising, but you should track the results nevertheless.

Provoke a Response with Reciprocal Communications

In addition to direct response advertising and public relations, a third highly effective method of obtaining marketing feedback literally comes from provoking a response so you can assess and measure the results. This allows you not only to follow the market, but to lead it.

A reciprocal communication has three elements: a statement thanking customers for their business; a request for customers to provide you with some information, usually by filling out a questionnaire; and the offer of an incentive for their efforts.

One of my clients is a group of physicians who send their patients a detailed questionnaire once a year. They thank patients for their trust and confidence, and then ask about the telephone performance of the staff, the ambience of the reception area and treatment rooms, the professionalism of the doctors and assistants, how insurance claims are handled, if the office hours are convenient, who referred the patient, and more. To show their appreciation for the time it takes to complete the questionnaire, they offer a free medical screening, an informative book, or some other incentive which changes from year to year.

We send out an annual questionnaire to everyone who has bought *The Desktop Lawyer* software package. We thank them for their purchase, let them know that the revised edition is now available, and then ask for their help with future revisions. We ask what documents they use and don't use, plus what documents they've needed that we didn't include in the package. We let them know that when we receive the completed questionnaire, we'll send them a free copy of a valuable report we have recently put together. One year, the report was on tax reform strategies; another year it was a family will and trust audit.

The point is, we're not just listening and responding to the market, we're provoking a response from the market so we can more specifically adapt our products and services to meet their needs.

Listening Like a Hawk

Have you ever gone for a ride in a sailplane? When you break away from the tow plane, you're enveloped in a wonderful silence as you catch the air currents necessary to stay aloft. Cumulus clouds—the white billowy ones—usually indicate the presence of an upward air current, so you provoke that current by steering toward them. You'll know you've caught it when one of your wingtips goes up; you bank the plane and follow the current as long as you can. When you lose it, you look for another one.

You also pay attention to what's on the ground. If you're over flat, grassy fields, you're not likely to find an updraft. But if you're over a forested area with tall trees, you're likely to find lots of air currents, so you move toward those areas to provoke a response from them.

On a good day, with a sensitive pilot, sailplanes can stay in the air for hours, rising on the upward currents and finally gliding gently back to earth. Pilot your business the way you would pilot a sailplane—by staying sensitive to any movement and provoking a response that will tell you where your market is and how you should direct your company.

The point you should understand is that marketing is not just "talking." Yes, it's essential that you let your market know who you are, what makes you different, and how the market can participate with you. That is, after all, the essence of the marketing message.

But it is also essential that you listen. In fact, listen like a hawk. Listen with all pores open. Listen to the market talking to you as you pilot that sailplane—ever vigilant to that slight breath of wind beneath your wing that tells you about the updraft just ahead.

Remember, the first part of marketing is identifying your market; the second part is developing your marketing message and communicating it to your market through advertising, public relations, and provoking a response. We're ready now to take a look at the third part of marketing: sales and customer service. A lot of management theorists assign these two functions to Operations. But Operations, as you will learn later, is an expense, a function that costs you money. Sales and customer service are two functions that, if handled properly, will generate revenue, which means it is appropriate to place them under Marketing in your business structure.

Sales and Customer Service

"They've got a good product, but the pushy salesperson just turned me off."

"The reason I buy from them is that the salesperson seemed more concerned about satisfying my needs than earning a commission."

"They're customer service is terrible. Once they had my money, they forgot about me."

"I could get a better price elsewhere, but I go to them because they're customer service is excellent and that's important to me."

Over the years, you've probably said or heard a version of these lines and, whether you meant to or not, had an impact on the sales of the organization you were talking about. In most companies, the two most publicly visible departments are sales and customer service, and if these two groups aren't operating well, everything else you do won't mean much. Disseminating your marketing message through advertising and public relations is mass communication—you are reaching a broad group of people. The selling process narrows that down to a one-on-one experience, whether you go to the customer or the customer comes to you. Once the sale is made, customer service becomes paramount.

There is a very close connection between sales, customer service, and public relations. The comments people make about you and your company contribute to your public image and can affect future revenue. A personal recommendation is the best promotion you can have, and a vote of no confidence can cost you sales. So what are people really saying about you?

To keep the public perception positive, everyone on your staff—*everyone!*—should receive training in active listening and needs-satisfaction selling. It's a worthwhile investment to pick up the tab for these courses, and there are a lot of them out there to choose from. Or buy self-improvement books for your staff.

If you are in a retail situation, consider using "mystery shoppers" to evaluate your floor personnel. Conduct random post-purchase surveys to make sure sales were handled properly and to find areas where you can improve. And have a skilled customer service team in place to take over after the sale.

How your customers are treated is a direct reflection of your own attitudes and concerns. It's truly a top-down process. You've seen some companies that bend over backward to keep the customer happy. Prior to being sold, Jefferson Institute was one of those. Howard Ruff, the former owner and founder of the Ruff Organization, which was the institute's parent company, insisted that under no circumstances would a customer ever be dissatisfied with the products or services provided by the Jefferson Institute. Consequently, each individual within the organization went above and beyond the call of duty to satisfy the customers. Howard's feelings were continually communicated to everyone on the staff, and they respected those feelings and responded to them.

By contrast, there are companies that are so non–service oriented that it's apparent the employees just don't care. We've all been in hotels that were dirty or stores where clerks couldn't be bothered with helping us. But I'm convinced that people don't take jobs with the idea of seeing how many customers they can chase off; in fact, new employees are generally the most enthusiastic. What makes the difference? The message they get from management, and ultimately from the company's owner. That message must be consistent, and it must be that total customer satisfaction is essential to the success of the business.

Customer service is little more than at least being prepared to address customer complaints while they are still minor inconveniences, before they escalate into major problems, and at best using those communications as additional sales and revenue opportunities. Many people believe the best quality indicator is not how a company operates when things are going well, but how it operates when things go wrong. So the first step in effective customer service is letting each customer know you are prepared to resolve their problems.

If you are a retail operation, post signs with your customer service policy in conspicuous locations—and keep it simple. All the signs need to say is "We are committed to providing complete customer satisfaction. If there was anything about your visit today that was not to your liking, please see Mary Jones, our customer service manager."

If you provide delivery, insert a small card in each package that reads, "Thank you for your order. If you have any questions about the enclosed merchandise, please call John Smith at 555-4567." Avoid saying things like, "If you have any problems . . . ," because that suggests that you expect the customer will. But make sure that in the unlikely event that something isn't right, your customers know who to call to get the situation corrected.

Never tell your customers to just "call the management." Always give them a specific name to ask for. Ideally, one person should handle all your complaints, but that's not always practical. In that case, you can use a code instead of the name of a real person. You'll know when someone asks for "Robert Houseman," for example, that they have a customer support concern.

Most of the time, it will take very little effort to handle a problem. But you need to do more than just "fix" the situation. My sporting goods business has a large number of institutional accounts, and occasionally the product count in an order shipped might be off. Even though we check and double-check orders, once in a while we might be off a couple of softballs in an order of three thousand. That in itself is not a serious problem, and it's easy to fix. But to maintain our market position and preserve relations with the affected customer, we apply a set procedure to resolve any delivery problem. For example, if a customer is short a dozen Ping-Pong balls, he or she receives an immediate acknowledgment and an apology, and the missing merchandise is shipped promptly. And we don't quibble about who is right. The customer is right—even if we suspect they are wrong.

A complaint concerning the quality of your product is more sensitive. If what you sold is defective in some way, your first step should be to find out what the customer wants you to do. Sometimes a customer will tell you right away; other times, you may have to ask to make sure. But the simple statement "I'm sorry you are dissatisfied. What can we do to make things right?" will diffuse a customer's ire and set the stage for a rapid resolution. Does the customer want you to accept the merchandise back and issue a refund? That's a simple solution. Or would the customer prefer that you replace the item? Again, that's easy enough to do. And rarely do customers want you to do anything more than one of those two things.

So long as the customers' requests are reasonable, give them what they want and thank them for bringing the situation to your attention. Let them know you will take steps to prevent the problem from happening again, and that you appreciate their business and hope to serve them again soon. Chances are, you will.

Chapter Six Highlights

—Marketing is about difference, and understanding what makes you different is essential to success.

—Marketing consists of identifying your niche, communicating with it, and supporting the customers marketing produces.

—Analyze the market by reading trade and general publications, attending trade shows and conventions, and developing a customer profile.

—Your marketing message should have three parts: who you are, what makes you different, and how your potential customer can participate.

—There are three ways to communicate with your market: advertising, public relations, and reciprocal communication.

—There are two basic types of advertising: institutional and direct response.

—Institutional advertising is ineffective because it is not a complete marketing message and does not provide a vehicle for feedback or measurement.

—Direct response advertising is effective because it is a complete marketing message, it invites a specific action by the customer, and it produces results that can be analyzed and measured.

—Public relations is actually more effective than advertising and much less expensive.

—Money spent on direct response advertising and public relations is *not* an expense; it is an investment in revenue production.

—Provoke a response with reciprocal communications.

—Your attitude toward customer satisfaction will be reflected by every member of your organization.

—Have a system in place to handle your customers' minor inconveniences before they become major problems.

CHAPTER SEVEN

Product Development and Expansion

Marketing Your Company's Growth

"Marketing concepts have to go into the design of the product
... if the product isn't designed to be saleable, you are simply
not going to be successful in selling it. Think of your product
in marketing terms, not just in terms of how wonderful it is."

—Howard Ruff, author, lecturer, and publisher of *Ruff Times*

ONCE YOU HAVE ESTABLISHED your company as an extension of yourself,
a business entity built around your own needs and desires, you need
to develop a product. You may have already done this as you worked
through the personal, business, and market identification portions of
integrational processing. Product development is the natural next step,
and approaching it this way means your product will be consistent
with your market, your business, and yourself.

Develop Products That Will Be Accepted Within Your Market

One of the most important lessons you will ever learn about your
business is this: product development is a marketing issue. The traditional view places product development in the research and development department, which generally falls under Production on the
organizational chart. Maybe that's because corporate bureaucrats think
the repetition of the word "development" makes the association a

natural one. Maybe they're afraid to let anyone else get their hands on an idea if all the production details haven't been ironed out. Whatever the reason, in most companies products and services are created and then passed to Marketing with instructions to figure out how to sell them. And the marketing department will do the best they can with what they have.

But my friend Tom wasn't coming from Production when he realized there was a market for products to aid the hearing-impaired. Production was secondary. The primary issue was that he had identified a market with a particular need. Once he did that, he figured out a product that took care of that need. It was the same situation when Rebecca Matthias founded Mothers Work. She wasn't manufacturing maternity clothes. She was a professional woman who had been unable to find appropriate clothing when she was pregnant, and realized other women shared her frustrations. The production of maternity wear for career women came after the market was identified.

Conner Peripherals, the disk drive maker called America's fastest growing company by *Fortune* magazine, takes this idea even further. The company's business formula is sell, design, and build—in that order. They won't engineer a new product unless a buyer has already spoken for it. Conner Peripherals went from being a $1 million company to being a $1 billion company in just four years. Cofounder and Chief Executive Finis Conner obviously has a flair for marketing. But he doesn't do anything you can't do.

Howard Ruff used the same formula when he developed his newsletter, the *Ruff Times.* He wrote an exciting direct mail piece describing a wonderful publication that didn't exist yet. The actual newsletter was created around the specifications laid out in his marketing piece. He figured out what would be saleable, waited for the market to respond, and then created it.

Once you have accepted and begun operating on the premise that product development is a marketing issue, you can create a line of products or services that will be extremely profitable. Remember, with integrational processing, you can decide who your market is before you decide on a specific product. You understand yourself, you know what type of business you want to be in, you have defined your market, and now, based on your business and market identification, you develop a product. Tom wanted to start a business that would help the hearing-impaired. He decided his market would be individuals who are hearing-impaired and their family members. Then he developed a product consistent with his business mission statement and his market identification—and the product was a hit.

Every year, thousands of products are introduced that have no market. They are exciting and interesting only to the people who produce them. A large percentage of these products could have been successful if they had they been modified to meet the needs and desires of a given market. You need to go beyond identifying your market—you need to understand it. Remember, understanding your customers means knowing what motivates them to buy. Once you have that understanding, you will know what products are likely to be well received by your customer base. You acquire this information by conducting the necessary market research.

There's no secret to market research. You've done a great deal of it in identifying your market and developing your customer profile. The key is to learn everything you can about your existing market and how that market is likely to evolve in the future. Solid market research will help you expand your business both horizontally and vertically in ways that are virtually risk-free.

Shifting Your Center of Business

Just as the planet has a center of gravity, your company has a center of business—the strongest place in your market. So let's say you understand your market, you have created a current customer profile, and you have identified a product or service you can offer at a profitable level. You know where your center of business has traditionally been, but as you study your customer profile, you see that that center has moved. You may or may not be able to determine the reason, but what's important is that you've identified a trend and you can build your business in that direction.

Take the case of a coin laundry, which has been a popular vehicle for small business owners for decades. If you're in the business of operating a coin laundry, you'll invest your money in washing machines and dryers, soap dispensers, and maybe a soft drink and snack machine. You'll keep the place clean, well lit, and make sure everything functions properly. That's about all you'll do.

But if you're paying attention to your customer profile, you might spot a shift in the center of your business that tells you that maybe you're not really in the coin laundry business anymore. You might see that your customers are primarily single people, and that your laundry is providing them with an opportunity to meet and mingle while they wash their clothes.

In that case, your center of business has shifted from providing a place where people do their laundry to providing a meeting place for singles. That shift demands different products and services, so you respond by installing a more comfortable lounge area, some arcade games, and a few more vending machines. If you have several coin laundries around town, you might notice that the ones that are stronger are located in more upscale areas, where your customers want flavored mineral water and fancy little snacks made of "all natural" ingredients. Your center of business has shifted again, because now you're providing refreshments and entertainment to a young singles market—and all you started with was a coin laundry.

Remember, your market is always a moving target, and your customer profile is not a onetime project, it is a perpetual effort. Follow your market the way a sailplane follows air currents. Constantly listen to what your customers are and are not saying about what and why they buy. This is the only way your business will increase and ultimately replicate itself.

I suggest treating your business like an organic vegetable garden—that is, "grow your business" naturally. When you pull the weeds by hand instead of using chemicals to kill them, you can really see how each plant is doing. When you maintain an accurate, up-to-date customer profile, you will instinctively know if your center of business is where it needs to be, or if you need to adjust it. Move when and where the marketplace pulls you, rather than forcing your will on the marketplace.

Horizontal and Vertical Expansion

Product development and expansion are fundamentally one and the same. You expand your business by expanding the products or services it offers, and you do that horizontally, vertically, or both.

Horizontal expansion broadens your customer base, providing you with the same amount of per capita income, or sales, from a wider market. You simply find more customers like the ones you have.

Vertical expansion gives you more income, or sales, from the same market. You persuade the customers you have to spend more money.

Susan, a massage therapist, was looking for a way to increase her income when she attended my Small Business Intensive in Dallas. She was doing an average of four massages a day for thirty minutes each and charging forty dollars per session. When I asked who her customer was, she said she didn't know. But when she thought about it, she realized the largest percentage of her business was corporate executives looking to reduce the effects of stress. She was located near a college and was advertising on the campus, yet only a handful of her customers were students.

Obviously, the first way she could begin to increase her income was to redirect her advertising efforts so she could reach more of the people who fit her primary customer profile. She stopped running ads in the campus newspaper and got a list of all the chief executive, financial, and operating officers in the Dallas-Fort Worth area. Then she put together a marketing presentation geared to helping them reduce stress on the job. Because a customer profile allows you to identify and attract other people just like your existing customers, Susan was able to expand horizontally because she knew whom she was targeting.

If all Susan did was broaden her customer base, her income would definitely increase, but her potential would always be capped by the number of hours in a day she could work. She can remove that cap with vertical expansion. When she has a customer on the table, she has a captive audience for the thirty or sixty minutes it takes to do the massage. She can sell an assortment of additional products, so long as they are consistent with the product or service that attracted her customer in the first place. Those products might include audio cassette tapes or compact disks of background music designed to relieve tension. She can promote the music by playing it during the massages. In her treatment room, she can include a display of exercise videos, lotions, vitamins, minerals, and special stress-reduction tablets, strategically positioned in the customer's direct line of vision. As she talks to her customers, she can recommend specific products appropriate to their situations.

Susan's customer profile has allowed her to identify the need that prompts clients to come to her in the first place. Armed with that information, she can add products and services that complement what she does to satisfy the original need, resulting in a higher volume of sales. The client who was spending twenty dollars for a massage is now likely to walk out with a ten-dollar audio tape and a fifteen-dollar bottle of vitamins—and Susan has practiced vertical expansion.

If you operate a dog grooming salon, your vertical expansion could—and should—include a wide array of pet care products and related novelty items, but don't expect to make much money by offering professional desk accessories. While you might be able to sell calendars with cute animal photographs, leave the elaborate planners and organizers in the office supply stores.

The key to successful expansion is to control it in a vertical or horizontal direction. When you hear that a company has failed because they expanded "too fast," it's more likely they attempted to expand without considering their customer profile, and added products or services that were inconsistent with their mission statement. Rather than expanding organically, they probably tried to force growth by pushing outside influences on the company—and that won't work.

Your market is made up of customers—the people who buy from you. Do you know what happens when you don't listen to your market? Have you ever heard of a car called the Edsel?

Remember, profitable horizontal and vertical expansion is based on knowing your customer and responding accordingly.

Chapter Seven Highlights

—Product development is a marketing issue, not a production issue.

—The center of your business should be flexible so you can follow the market when it moves.

—Product development and expansion are fundamentally the same.

—Horizontal expansion lets you broaden your customer base.

—Vertical expansion lets you realize greater revenue from existing customers.

—The key to any successful expansion effort is staying consistent with your market.

CHAPTER EIGHT

Test Marketing
Fine-Tune Before You Roll Out

"In order to try whether a vessel be leaky, we first prove it with water before we trust it with wine."

—Charles Caleb Colton, English clergyman

EVEN WITH THE GREATEST idea and the best planning, concept and reality can be two very different things. Test marketing is essential for the success of any business idea. Understand that most products are *viable,* but you need to know under what circumstances they will be *profitable.* And this is not the time to rely heavily on intuition or the buying patterns of your friends and relatives. Intuition is certainly worthwhile, and your friends and relatives may possibly become part of your customer base, but solid information is the most effective tool to use in creating your rollout parameters. So whenever possible, go for the unbiased facts and then make your decisions.

A wise approach to marketing—and one I don't take credit for, because it's taught by a number of experts—is "Ready, *fire!,* aim." You get ready, fire a shot to see where it's going to hit, then work on getting closer to your target.

Remember when I compared the shotgun to the rifle and then to the fencing foil? When you begin test marketing, you start with a shotgun, move up to a rifle, and then ultimately graduate to the very precise fencing foil. When you reach for your market with the fencing foil, you have determined the circumstances under which your product will be most profitable. You have discovered the best marketing strategy, the optimum price, a satisfying delivery system, and all the other details that will add up to a successful business.

You achieve this by testing, testing, testing, and the testing stage is critical in order to help you to verify the viability of your product or service, develop rollout parameters, and establish your criteria for success.

How to Test

There are four primary methods of testing, and you should use one or more of them for each product you introduce. Always remember that during the testing stage, your objective is to gather information. Don't concern yourself with profit at this point. The cost of testing is simply a cost of doing business. You need to know if your product and your marketing plan are going to work. You need feedback to determine what, if any, adjustments you should make to your original idea to improve market performance. You don't need profit right now, although in some test scenarios you might make a little money. But when you design your test to make a profit, or make it dependent on profits, you prejudice the results. And if you prejudice the results, they won't help you when you move from testing to rollout. You might fail and you might succeed, but you won't know why. So invest in testing, concentrate on the results, make modifications and changes, and ignore the opportunity for profit from the test process.

Surveys. Simply put, surveys are just a formal way of collecting opinions. You've probably participated in more surveys than you can count—especially during election years. And you've probably been known to use surveys to prove a point, quoting a poll, for example, that says 79 percent of the population shares your view. In test marketing, surveys are an excellent way to gain information before you actually start up your operation about how your business will likely be perceived.

Surveys can be conducted in person, by mail, over the phone, or even electronically, and are generally the least expensive way to test your market. They consist of two primary parts: market data (your questions) and respondent demographics (who is answering your questions).

The importance of the first section is obvious. You wouldn't be bothering with this whole exercise if you didn't need information. But remember most people have a relatively short attention span, so don't ask them any more questions than are absolutely necessary. Make the questions you do ask easy to answer, usually with either "yes" or "no," or perhaps multiple choice. Busy people will be more inclined to answer your survey if it's presented in a format that lets them do it quickly, and simple answers are easier to tabulate.

The second section is important because you need to know if the people responding to your survey are truly prospective customers. If your product is a high-priced luxury item for homeowners, you don't need to survey low-income renters. If your product is designed to be sold to other businesses, surveying homemakers is a waste of time. So end your survey with enough questions to identify your respondents accurately.

If you want to open an espresso bar in a kiosk in the middle of a major shopping mall, and you've determined that there is general market acceptability for the concept, there's an excellent chance you'll make a profit. Still, you want to test. So you decide to do a survey.

Arm yourself with a clipboard, a stack of blank survey forms, and head to the mall. After getting permission from the mall management, politely stop people and say, "May I ask you a few questions? I promise I won't sell you a thing, and it will only take three minutes of your time."

Your survey will look something like this:

SAMPLE SURVEY FORM

Date/Time_____

MARKET DATA

How often do you visit this mall?

3 times a week or more ____
1–2 times a week ____
2–3 times a month ____
1 time a month ____
less than 1 time a month ____

When you're here, how long do you usually stay (average length of visit)?

less than 1 hour ____
1–2 hours ____
2–3 hours ____
3–4 hours ____
4–5 hours ____
5–6 hours ____
more than 6 hours ____

How often do you have lunch in the mall?

3 times a week or more ____
1–2 times a week ____
2–3 times a month ____
1 time a month ____
less than 1 time a month ____

How often do you have other refreshments in the mall?

3 times a week or more ____
1–2 times a week ____
2–3 times a month ____
1 time a month ____
less than 1 time a month ____

What is the beverage you enjoy most frequently during mall visits?

Coffee ____
Hot tea ____
Soft drinks ____
Fruit juice ____
Other _____

Do you know what espresso is?

Yes ____
No ____

Have you ever tasted it?

Yes ____
No ____

Do you like it?

Yes ____
No ____
If no, why not?

_____

If it were available, would you drink it here?

Yes ____
No ____
How often? _____

Would you enjoy some type of pastry or other snack with your espresso?

Yes ____
No ____

Would you consider $1.50 per cup an acceptable price for an espresso?

Yes ____
No ____

If no, is $1.50 per cup too high _____
    or too low _____?

RESPONDENT DEMOGRAPHICS

Age:
    under 25 _____
    25–35 _____
    36–45 _____
    46–55 _____
    56–65 _____
    over 65 _____

Sex: M ____ F ____

Occupation: _____

Annual household income:
  under $10,000 ___
  $10,000–$20,000 ___
  $21,000–$30,000 ___
  $31,000–$40,000 ___
  $41,000–$60,000 ___
  $61,000–$75,000 ___
  over $75,000 ___

Once you've completed the surveys, it's time to catalog the information. Measure the responses you received to each question. What percentage of the people you talked to knew what espresso is? How many of them said they would drink it if it was available? How many would enjoy something sweet along with it? How did they react to your suggested price?

This survey will not only help you determine whether or not an espresso bar will be profitable in this particular location, but also guide you in selecting related products for sale—pastries and donuts, for example—and assist you in setting prices.

When I began developing the *Successful Living Library,* a collection of audio and video tapes on a variety of business and financial subjects offered through The Open University, I was traveling around the country teaching the Small Business Intensive and the Family Wealth Building Seminar. The final version of the *Library* was the result of surveys I distributed at each workshop. Some of the questions I asked were the following: Does this workshop contain the type of information you've been looking for? Would you be interested in learning about other subjects through an audio or video tape format? Do you have a VCR? Please rank the following subjects from 1 to 20 in order of their level of interest for you. (And I gave them a list of subjects I thought would most likely be of interest.) How much would you be willing to pay for a one-hour audio tape of this nature? For a one-hour video tape?

I distributed the survey at different times during different seminars. Sometimes I would hand it out at the beginning, sometimes at the break or at lunch, sometimes at the end. That allowed me to see how much the seminar itself was biasing the results, which turned out to be a substantial amount. People who completed the survey at the end of the seminar tended to be interested in subjects that did not have a strong appeal to people who completed the survey at the beginning. This pattern was so strong that it had to be attributed to the content of the seminar.

These surveys gave me an understanding of the potential level of general market acceptance for the *Library* as well as some very specific information about subject and price. My out-of-pocket expenses were only about a hundred dollars—primarily the cost of printing the form. And the responses told me what I needed to know to avoid a very costly mistake. Indeed, the *Successful Living Library* has been a very well-received and successful product for me over the years.

There's not a lot of difference between surveys and interviews. In fact, interviews can be considered almost a verbal survey, and work equally well for test marketing purposes. In a sense, they work even better because the interviewing function provides for interactive communication.

An important point to keep in mind about both surveys and interviews is that they have limited value. Though they will provide you with some information, they should not be weighted too heavily in your evaluations. The problem with them is that they require no financial commitment on the part of the person who is responding. Sure, they said they'd buy espresso at $1.50 a cup, but will they really? Sure, they told me they'd like to see a seminar on real estate investment strategies, but can I count on them to be in the audience when I teach the session? We don't know for sure.

You've probably heard the phrase "Until they buy, it's all a lie." That might sound cynical, but keep it in mind and don't rely too heavily on data you collect without a purchase on the part of the respondent. Nonetheless, surveys and interviews are an important part of testing (or tapping) the market.

Limited Objectives Testing. This type of testing is actually a partial implementation of your marketing plan to gather results based on specific limitations. With limited objectives testing, you can determine the effectiveness of the marketing plan you have developed for your product and make any appropriate adjustments before you launch a full-scale campaign.

Let's say you've determined that your business mission statement is to develop outdoor sports products that will help busy people maximize and enjoy their limited leisure time. Your first product is going to be a compact fishing kit—a rod and reel that folds small enough to be carried in a glove compartment, briefcase, or purse. With the compact fishing kit, fishing enthusiasts will be prepared to fish anytime the opportunity arises, without carrying around a lot of bulky gear.

This product is appropriate for both your business identification and market identification. Now you need a potential universe to test it on.

During the course of your market research, you discover a publication called *Bassmaster Magazine.* Over 500,000 people subscribe to this magazine, which consists largely of photographs of bass with fishing hooks in their open mouths. If ever there was a potential universe of people who would buy the compact fishing kit, it's *Bassmaster Magazine* subscribers. You contact the publication's marketing department and arrange to purchase 5,000 randomly selected names from their mailing list to send your direct mail brochure to. For our example, we'll say your total cost—list, printing, and mailing—is $0.50 per piece. You now have $2,500 invested in this limited objectives test, and you're ready to measure the results. Your response rate is 1 percent, or 50 orders for the compact fishing kit at $20 each, making your total revenue $1,000. From that, deduct $200 for the cost of the product, and your contribution to overhead is $800.

Was the test a failure? Certainly not! It was a tremendous success. You now know that for every $2,500 you put out under those parameters, you'll get back $800—not the formula for profitability you were looking for. The $1,700 it ultimately cost you to conduct this test was a good investment, because now you know you do not want to use this marketing strategy on all of the more than 500,000 people who subscribe to *Bassmaster.*

There are two very important things to remember about limited objectives testing. First, as in all types of test marketing, do not test for profit, test for results. Test to gain information that will allow you to establish the parameters that will most likely assure your success. And second, do not extend the implications of the conclusion. What I mean by that is that you shouldn't apply the results gained under one particular set of circumstances to another set of circumstances. What this test told you was that one mailing to *Bassmaster* subscribers of a specific brochure, with your product priced at $20, generated enough revenue to cover 32 percent of the cost of the mailing. It didn't tell you whether you have a viable product or not. You need more information before you can determine that. You may need to reconsider your price structure or your test universe.

So you make the assumption that people who are so dedicated to fishing they are willing to spend $20 on the compact fishing kit would also be willing to pay $30 for it. You do a mailing to another 5,000 names at a $30 price point. This time your response rate doubles, making your total revenue $3,000. Subtract product cost of $400, and you have a contribution to overhead of $2,600. What does this tell you? Remember, you're not concerned with the profitability of the test. What you've learned is that $30 is a far more effective price point than $20.

When Chuck Givens started selling his *Money Strategies* program, he priced it at $45 and got mixed results. Sales volume improved when he raised it to $95. But he didn't get the best results until he started selling the program at $245. Why? Who knows—but I suspect that at $245 there was a perceived value that was lacking when the price was $45. Had Chuck decided, based on the mixed results generated from marketing at the lower price, that *Money Strategies* was not a viable product, he would have been quite wrong. By testing the price, he was able to determine his product's intrinsic profitability.

When I first offered the Entrepreneur Intensive, which was the predecessor of the Small Business Intensive, I priced it at $75, and the response rate was dismal. When I raised the price to $195, the response rate increased, and it went even higher when I upped the price to $295.

The Desktop Lawyer is a collection of legal forms and checklists designed to walk readers through every conceivable business transaction they might encounter. When I first started selling it, I wasn't sure how to price it, so I started at $195. Sales were good, but they got better when I gradually increased the price to $395. When the price went up to $495, and then to $595, sales leveled, but I was making $100 per unit more. (A side note: *The Desktop Lawyer* has evolved from two large books of forms to a stand-alone, menu-driven software program, which currently retails for $139.95.)

Remember that, in addition to price, your universe is also subject to testing. For the compact fishing kit, you used *Bassmaster* subscribers, but you could have used any universe. And it could be that the universe of *Bassmaster* subscribers was not an appropriate market for your product. It might be that they had no need for the compact fishing kit, that they are so dedicated to fishing that they walk around all day with a standard fishing rod in their hands. *Bassmaster* subscribers might have been an inappropriate universe; something like *Field and Stream* readers might work better.

So in addition to testing for price, you should also consider testing with a separate universe. The compact fishing kit sells better at $30 than it does at $20—but only to *Bassmaster* subscribers. Will sales increase if you raise the price to $40? You won't know until you test. Will the same percentage of *Field and Stream* readers be willing to pay $20 for this product? You won't know until you test.

A standard testing strategy to consider is a split run test. Buy 5,000 names and mail to half at one price and half at another price. Or test your marketing package by sending half the names one brochure and half another brochure. You may even want to send half by first class mail and half by bulk mail. Though bulk mail is less expensive, you may find that if you mail first class, you get a higher response rate that more than makes up for the additional cost. You won't know until you test.

But always, as you test, remember never to extend the significance of the conclusion past the raw data you've produced. Don't assume a different set of circumstances will produce the same results, and test as many different angles as you can.

General Mills, one of the largest non-franchised restaurant operations in the United States, made what was probably the biggest mistake in their corporate history by extending the significance of their conclusion. They bought a chain called Good Earth Restaurants, which, up until that point, had operated only in California. The restaurants in the original purchase were substantially profitable. General Mills test marketed the concept in other Southern California cities and expanded the number of restaurants in that area. Most were by and large successful. Based on that performance, General Mills decided it had a winner and rapidly expanded Good Earth Restaurants from Southern California to the East Coast. That was their mistake. With only minor exceptions, Good Earth Restaurants bombed.

What General Mills did was extend the significance of the results past the original universe they tested on. A more appropriate expansion would have been to build a few of these restaurants in strategic locations—maybe one in Birmingham, one in Baltimore, and one in Chicago—and then examine the results. In that way, they probably would have recognized that the general public was not ready in the early 1980s to embrace a mainstream dining facility with the image of a health food restaurant. They could have cut their losses, closed the unsuccessful test restaurants, and made a decision on what to do with the remaining Southern California locations. Those hypothetical losses would have been far less than the actual ones incurred when dozens of Good Earth Restaurants across the country were closed. General Mills also could have expanded only in markets with the same type of customer base as the Southern California areas where the restaurants were doing so well. While that might have limited the number of Good Earth restaurants, which is contrary to the General Mills goal of turning each restaurant in their stable into a national chain, at least that strategy would have maintained profitability and preserved the chain.

So, at the risk of repeating myself, let me say again: never extend the significance of the results past the raw data you've accumulated.

Temporary Associations. This is another form of limited objectives testing. In a temporary association, you can gain a significant amount of feedback without committing yourself fully to an organizational structure that has not yet proven its profitability.

When we first got into the sporting goods business, we weren't sure if we wanted to include trophies in our product line. We knew we didn't want to include boating and marine supplies, but there was always a chance consumer demand would be high enough to justify carrying them. So I went to one of the largest trophy shops in town and asked if they'd like to put a trophy department in the store. I did the same thing with a local boat dealer and marine supply house. We provided the floor space, they provided the merchandise, and we split the profits fifty-fifty. All the participants knew that at any given time, we might convert their departments to ones that were store-owned, or we might simply terminate our agreement.

On the basis of these two temporary associations, I was able to determine that I would go ahead with my own full trophy department, but I was correct in not wanting to sell boating and marine supplies. After a reasonable test period, the boating and marine supplies were removed and the contracted trophy department was replaced with our own line of trophies. Temporary association saved us a lot of time and energy.

Millie's Millinery is an example of a temporary association from a slightly different angle. Millie wanted a fine millinery shop in The Plaza, Kansas City's elite shopping district. She approached Hall's

Department Store and worked out an agreement where she set up her operation in a small area of their store and paid a percentage of her sales as rent. She was immediately exposed to a substantial amount of foot traffic with very little invested other than in her inventory, giving her the opportunity to test market which products would sell in that particular region.

She started with what she considered to be high-end goods. In short order, she learned that her concept of high-end merchandise was actually the low end of what was selling. Items priced at three to four times what she had anticipated were being snapped up. Millie had wisely limited her original inventory. Because she didn't have a lot of money tied up in merchandise that either wouldn't sell at all, or wouldn't sell for as great a profit as other merchandise, it was easy to add those higher-priced, more profitable products that would sell easily and quickly.

When Millie eventually moved to her own shop, she did so with two major advantages: she knew exactly what would sell, because her testing had already been done, and she had an existing customer base that knew her and would follow her.

Had she started with her own store instead of with the temporary association, she would have had to worry about how to generate the foot traffic. What's more, she would have inventoried her store based on what she thought would sell and then found she was wrong with about 75 percent of the merchandise. Not only would she have had to take significant markdowns and possibly a bath on those items, but also she wouldn't have satisfied the customer base she was attempting to reach.

In Millie's case, a temporary association clearly allowed her to verify the viability of her product, develop rollout parameters, and establish the criteria for success—all without substantial economic risk.

An excellent resource for temporary associations is product fairs. I once had an idea for fast-food crepes called Crepes-To-Go. Crepes were a very "in" food item at the time, and food sold by street vendors has always been popular. I envisioned combining these two winning concepts with a limited selection of crepes sold from carts strategically placed in the downtown business district of Orlando. I developed a business identification and a market identification. But I couldn't get the carts licensed in Orlando, and that's where I made my first mistake. I didn't follow my initial business mission statement, and I decided to go with sit-down locations. Having actual restaurants rather than the carts significantly increased the overhead and the necessary investment. It also meant that a more varied menu was required. But I didn't think that would be a problem, so I moved into the testing stage, where I made another series of test marketing mistakes.

I began by conducting taste testings in my office, where the crepes were freshly prepared in an oven and served promptly. (I have a full kitchen in my office.) They were delicious; everybody loved them and said they would buy them. So I further tested by setting up a booth in a food fair at the civic center in Orlando.

This particular fair attracted most of the restaurant operations in town, with their own exhibits, offering the best they had to offer in order to entice you into their restaurants later. Attendees roamed around sampling an incredible variety of food, from spare ribs to egg rolls to fish sticks.

So here we were, participating in this food fair to determine the viability of the concept of a fast-food restaurant specializing in crepes. I had a fellow who spoke with a charming French accent dressed up in a French chef's outfit (he was really from Liverpool, England, but who cared?) standing in our booth. As we sold the crepes, he would interview the customers to see how they liked them. The response was overwhelming. Though the menu was limited to a ham-and-cheese entrée crepe and a cherry dessert crepe, the people attending the fair loved them. During the course of the weekend, we made a profit of $4,000.

From the feedback we received on our "French chef's" surveys and from the sales figures, we decided that Crepes-To-Go would be a hit. I used the tremendous response from the food fair as justification to move into a rapid expansion mode, and we built three restaurants.

I was wrong.

In the process, I learned the third rule of limited objectives testing, one that I hadn't realized: when you are testing, make sure you simulate the exact same conditions that will be a part of your normal business operation.

What I wanted from the food fair test was a profitable endeavor. I wanted the customers to accept the crepes, to enjoy them, and to come back for more. So we slaved over those crepes to make them just right. But the concept of Crepes-To-Go was a fast-food operation where each dish would be quickly made and ready in less than a minute after the customer placed an order.

Was the food fair a success? It depends on your perspective. Yes, we made a profit, but profit is not a consideration of the testing process. The response to the survey was wonderful and encouraging, but the product those people were eating was not the product they would get at an actual Crepes-To-Go. In the normal restaurant operation, which we did not simulate either at the food fair or when we did taste testings in the office, we discovered all kinds of problems maintaining the temperature of the ingredients. We were promising fast food, but if you try to keep most ingredients hot all day, they turn to mush. So we kept them cold. But how could we go from cold to hot in less than a minute? With a microwave, of course. But have you ever microwaved a crepe?

Have you ever eaten a Frisbee?

Those crepes sailed. They floated. But they didn't get eaten.

No, the food fair was not a success. It was a failure, and for more reasons than just the cooking method.

Not only did we test incorrectly, but we even botched another important part of testing: simulating the same location. Particularly in a restaurant or retail operation, location is critical. When considering a site for your business, examine the broad geographic characteristics of your market as well as the accessibility of the facility. In Southern California, the Good Earth Restaurants were a reflection of that universe. In Orlando, Florida, they were not. A dinner theater in the downtown district of a midsize city might have a difficult time attracting patrons if parking is a problem. Locate the theater in a strip shopping center where you have lots of available parking, and you have a completely different story.

For fast-food crepes at a food fair, the audience is virtually captive. Will those people go out of their way to stop at a freestanding restaurant? Unfortunately, I didn't bother to find that out before I built three of them.

In this endeavor, I failed to follow my original business mission statement, I failed to test properly, and I drew inaccurate conclusions from the tests I did conduct. I broke my own rules, and I paid dearly for it. Of all the businesses I've ever been involved with, only one was a failure.

Crepes-To-Go was not a mere failure, it was an absolute disaster.

It took me eighteen months to plan the business. It took me three months to destroy it.

The rules for limited objectives testing, whether by temporary association, mail order, or some other method, are simple and essential:

- Test for results, not profits.
- Never extend the significance of the results past the raw data.
- Make sure you simulate exact operating conditions.

Implementation. The final way of testing is by actual implementation. While this may sound as if I'm giving you a way to skip test marketing, it's important that you understand that you are not ready to go to the real implementation stage, which would be the full operation of your business. Instead, you are using implementation as a testing device to acquire information. This is an option for test marketing only when it is not any more expensive than the test itself. Sometimes a limited objectives test will be as expensive, or even more so, than simply putting your full marketing plan in motion. The difference between implementation testing and the implementation stage are the rules of limited objectives testing.

For example, the investment required to put on a seminar is nominal, so when Chuck Givens began testing his financial seminars, he started with a small ad in the newspaper announcing the topic, location, and price—and he actually put on the seminar. The next time, he changed the ad somewhat. Then he changed the price. He was implementing his seminar programs, but he was really testing, researching the parameters for success. From his testing, he was able to determine the most effective advertising campaign, the most profitable pricing structure, and all the other details that made Givens seminars the impressive experience they are.

I did the same thing in the early days of The Open University, with the Small Business Intensive. I used traditional testing methods to evaluate my marketing strategy, but when it came to the seminar itself, the most efficient way to test was to just do it and then evaluate the response from the participants.

Testing by implementation provided Lori Meade Caldwell with a method to prove the value of her seminar and events coordinating business, Main Events, to prospective clients. Lori had been the coordinator of my seminar company for a number of years, and had also worked in similar capacities for other organizations. She used integrational processing to develop Main Events, and then approached a major seminar promoter. The success of Main Events depended on catching a sizable client. This promoter, as Lori expected, resisted the idea of using her, because they had staff members in place to do exactly what Lori was offering to do. They were already paying salaries; why pay an outside consultant?

Lori knew they had an upcoming seminar series that would require booking ten hotels in ten cities around the country. She offered them the following proposition: when their employees had done the best job possible and negotiated satisfactory contracts, they were to contact her with the details. She would take that information and book hotels of the same or higher quality for less money. She would take one-half of whatever money she saved them as her fee. If she couldn't save them any money, it wouldn't cost them anything. On the other hand, if she *could* save them money, they would pay her one-half the savings and contract with her for future events.

Obviously, the seminar promoter couldn't lose. Lori was hired, and ended up earning more on booking those ten hotels on a test basis than she would have if they had agreed to pay her standard fee. Testing by implementation not only earned her a substantial amount of money, but she gained a client who also provided her with recommendations and referrals. That was several years ago; today, Lori has taken what she learned in creating and building Main Events and is applying that knowledge to a very successful bed and breakfast she runs with her husband in Albuquerque.

Keep On Testing

A final point on test marketing: never become so confident about your product or marketing strategy that you skip over this process. It's easy to get so caught up in a product you believe in that you can't step back and see the product and your company as others do. But without that objective view, any success you experience will be purely accidental.

Testing provides you with the necessary data to market your business's products and services to their maximum advantage. Proper testing and analysis of the results can also prevent you from making some expensive mistakes, like my Crepes-To-Go fiasco. Sometimes it's the testing stage that actually propels you into full operations, as with Millie's Millinery and Main Events.

Once you actually rollout and are in full operation, keep on testing. Testing will give you feedback you need to make sure your company continues to follow your market. The first edition of *The Desktop*

Lawyer had approximately 250 pages in a notebook; the current edition is a stand-alone, menu-driven software program with elaborate support documentation. All that additional information is in response to what my market has told me through testing that it needs.

Testing is an ongoing process both for existing products and for modifications and expansions in your product line.

Is there any time when you would be justified in not conducting test marketing?

No.

Now that your tests have produced the information you need to rollout your product or service, it's time to move on to fulfillment services.

Chapter Eight Highlights

—Test marketing helps you verify the viability of your product or service, develop rollout parameters, and establish the criteria for success.

—The four primary methods of testing are surveys, limited objectives testing, temporary associations, and implementation.

—The value of a test increases significantly when the test respondent must make a financial commitment.

—Do not test for profits; test for results.

—Do not extend the significance of the conclusion past the raw data produced by the test.

—Test the price of your product and the universe you are marketing to.

—When you test, simulate the exact operational considerations that will be a part of your normal business.

CHAPTER NINE

Fulfillment Services
Getting Your Product to Market

THE SECOND LEG of your business structure is fulfillment services, or getting your product or service to the market. As a key element in any business, fulfillment services consist of distribution and delivery.

It's important you understand the difference between the two. Distribution is the way you sell, or the way products get to different market groups. Delivery is the way products are physically moved, or the way the marketplace gets products to the ultimate consumer.

Distribution Systems

Your distribution system should allow you to reach as many different customer bases as possible. We'll talk more about this in chapter thirteen, when we discuss add-on revenue sources as one of the critical elements of profitability. But first, let's take a look at your basic options for distribution and delivery. As you read, remember these are "mix and match" components. They are not mutually exclusive, but can be combined to provide you with a smooth-riding vehicle to success and profitability.

Retail. In a retail operation, you sell to the general public who comes to you to purchase goods and services. Consequently, you must communicate with your market in such a way that they are motivated to come to you to buy. Your location may be in an office building, a shopping center, or a regional mall. As a rule, home-based businesses are not candidates for retail distribution due to zoning restrictions.

There is a growing trend toward mobile businesses, but they are still retail operations. The difference is that, instead of your customer driving to you, you drive to your customer. Popular mobile businesses include small animal veterinary care, automobile repair, bicycle repair, accounting and other professional services, and interior decorating.

Franchise. Franchising can be a blessing, a curse, or a combination of the two for an entrepreneur. Once you have created a successful enterprise, franchising provides you with a method of duplicating your operation at a lower risk level by setting up agreements with local independent dealers. Those dealers—or franchisees—operate under your corporate name, and will help you reach a broader number of customer bases faster and more economically than you probably could without them.

The difference between a franchised and a non-franchised operation is not always readily apparent to an outside observer, and there are as many different franchise agreements as there are opportunities. In the context of a distribution system, franchising is simple and efficient. You distribute to the franchisee, and the franchisee distributes to the market.

A good number of businesses are capable of being franchised, and you should consider developing your business concept as if you were planning to franchise it, regardless of your true intention. This approach allows you to, as Michael E. Gerber says, work *on* your business, not *in* it. If your business is built around a system, rather than individuals, it can be operated by just about anyone. Systems are easy to duplicate; it's a lot more difficult with people.

The point is, if you create a system, then you've created a business. If you don't create a system, then all you've done is find yourself a job where you pay your own FICA and insurance. If your business won't work without the presence of a particular key person, usually the owner, then you don't have a business, you have a job. And you can't sell a job as you can a business.

I did tell you that behind every successful business is a strong personality, and that's true. These successful businesses are systems that operate without the actual physical presence of that strong personality. The late Ray Kroc's personality still shines through every McDonald's restaurant in the world—not because he spent time behind the grill cooking hamburgers, but because he created a system that just about anybody could operate profitably. Gerber addresses this concept in his book, *The E-Myth,* which should be required reading for any business owner.

Let's take a look at the other side of franchises: the people who buy them. If you are in the market for a franchise, you will become a part of a distribution system that is tremendously popular and healthy. Over half a million franchised business outlets represent more than two thousand companies operating in the United States alone. Don't be overwhelmed by the abundance of choices. Use integrational processing to find a franchise that "fits" you, your finances, your personality, and your lifestyle. Then research the franchisor carefully and completely before making a final decision.

The major advantage of buying a franchise over starting your own independent business is a larger measure of security. Using the franchisor's proven business plan maximizes the potential for success and minimizes the risk. At the same time, you lose some independence. If you don't like working within someone else's system, if you are intent on doing things your own way, being a franchisee is not for you.

Multilevel Marketing. Multilevel marketing, also known as matrix or network marketing, provides a massive distribution system that usually manages to remain very personal and friendly no matter how large the company gets. You recruit distributors, who sell products and who recruit other distributors, who sell products and recruit other distributors and so on. Besides making a profit on merchandise by buying wholesale and selling retail, each distributor gets a percentage, or an override, on the sales of everyone they sign up as distributors. That percentage may increase along with the size of their "downline"— the term used to describe the distributors they have recruited.

The distribution structure of MLM companies varies, but it's possible for the company to fill one order consisting of merchandise that has actually been purchased by twenty, thirty, or even more people. That would happen if distributors made their purchases from the company for sale to numerous other customers. Distributors also collect product orders from everyone in their downline and turn in one large order to the company.

Some MLM companies have a special category of distributor who stocks merchandise at the local level. Other distributors buy from that special distributor, instead of directly from the company. The efficiency advantage is obvious: rather than process countless numbers of small, individual orders, the company only has to process a select number of large orders.

You'll recognize the names of some incredibly successful multilevel operations: Amway, Mary Kay Cosmetics, and Pre-Paid Legal Services. You can check out multilevel opportunities by contacting the Direct Selling Association at (202) 293-5760.

Catalog. An increasing number of Americans are finding catalog shopping a convenient alternative to retail stores. Catalog companies usually operate on a direct mail basis, but many retail stores supplement their shop distribution with catalogs. The major advantage of a catalog distribution system is that it requires minimal overhead. You can create a substantial catalog business from your home without a major investment.

Tom's company, which offered products for the hearing-impaired, was a catalog business. His catalog was not extensive; with his particular market niche, it didn't have to be. He stocked a few products, all of which were small items easily stored in his garage. Orders for those items were filled and taken to UPS for shipping. He arranged for his suppliers to ship products he did not stock directly to his customers.

At Braxton Recreation Company, we have thousands of items in our inventory, but list only twenty-four seasonal items in a catalog we send out quarterly. That small catalog is very effective, but it would be equally effective if we stocked only the products we featured in it. Catalogs are an attractive, efficient distribution device regardless of how you handle your inventory.

Catalog companies are attractive opportunities from more than just an operational viewpoint. Changes in our demographics and overall society mean more people have less time to spend in stores, so the appeal of shopping at home from a catalog is increasing. Not only that, it's much easier to entice a prospective customer to flip through the pages of a specialty catalog than it is to coax them into their cars to drive to a retail center and browse through a specialty store. It also follows that retail distribution systems are naturally limited by geography; a catalog operation has no such restrictions.

Another advantage of a catalog company over a retail store is that you can get started with less inventory, which means a lower up-front investment. If you arrange for your suppliers to ship for you, you may not even have to pay for certain merchandise until you have sold it.

As mailing list brokers continue to refine their targeting capabilities, the opportunities for specialty catalogs increase. You can purchase mailing lists for people whose hobby is gourmet cooking, or whose annual income is above $50,000, or who have certain types of pets, or who fall into just about any specific category or combination of categories. You don't have to compete with Lillian Vernon, L. L. Bean, or Lands' End—although these are excellent examples of companies that started out small and grew to be industry leaders. With a catalog operation, a small company can mean big profits.

Distributorship. Distributorships are most common in industrial or business-to-business environments. Distributors sell merchandise that is generally of one specific type or category, and often they carry several items that will do the same job. For example, a local plumbing supply company may represent a variety of manufacturers of fixtures, many of which compete against one another. It's also easy to operate a distributorship from your home; all you need are your catalogs and maybe a few samples.

Jobber and Wholesaler. Jobbers and wholesalers buy in bulk from the manufacturer or importer and then resell to the retailer. Rack jobbers will set up displays in retail stores; the merchandise is sold on consignment, and the jobber's primary responsibility is to make sure the racks stay full. Items commonly sold by this method are videotapes (sales and rentals), snack foods, panty hose, magazines, and more.

Often referred to as the "middleman," jobbers and wholesalers offer retailers a valuable service. They generally represent a number of manufacturers and can supply the retailer with merchandise more easily and efficiently than if the retailer dealt with each manufacturer individually. Volume buying helps keep their purchase price down and contributes to profit.

Broker. A broker works as an independent agent bringing buyers and sellers together. The broker is paid on commission, generally by the seller, although that may vary with specific agreements.

• • •

This is only a partial list of the distribution systems that are available. You may even develop a system of your own by blending the characteristics of two or more existing formal systems with your own needs. Also, your business may take advantage of several distinct distribution systems to reach a broad range of customer bases.

When Dad and I started the first sporting goods store in 1971, it was as a retail operation. It didn't occur to me to investigate other distribution methods until we received a bid request from the school board of Dade County, Florida, for three thousand basketballs. At the time, we were selling approximately thirty basketballs a year retail.

I called Penn Athletic, a basketball supplier at the time, and told them about the bid request. They had been looking for an opportunity to gain a share of the Florida market, which was dominated by Seamco, one of Penn's competitors. Together we reached an agreement on a price that would allow us to make a profit. I mailed in the proposal, and a few weeks later we were notified that we had been awarded the bid. I sent a purchase order to Penn, who drop-shipped the balls directly to the Dade County school board.

My investment was a few telephone calls and the time it took to complete the proposal; my profit was about $1,300. Not a bad return—in fact, I really liked doing business that way. And it made sense to me that if I could do it once, I could do it again.

If the Dade County school board purchased basketballs in those quantities, it seemed safe to assume that other school boards were doing the same thing. So I sent out a request to every school board in the state to be put on their bid list. This, by the way, is a classic example of horizontal expansion: I had identified a customer and went to work on attracting similar customers. It was also a great opportunity for vertical expansion. After all, if school systems were buying basketballs, they were probably also buying baseballs and footballs and bats and helmets and so on—all items available through my store at different times of the year.

Not only did I get on their bid lists, but we developed the small seasonal catalog I mentioned earlier. Our catalog was nothing more elaborate than a three-panel brochure that was mailed quarterly to over four thousand institutions in the state. It helped us eventually become the largest institutional distributor of athletic goods in the state of Florida, a position we continue to maintain.

Our third level of distribution came about when I realized that because of our institutional sales, our vendors were offering us pricing that would allow us to resell items to other retailers at a 30 to 50 percent margin. Most retailers were like us before we got the first bid on basketballs—they were buying well under a hundred balls each year. But once we developed an institutional customer base, we were buying between ten and fifteen thousand balls per year. Our sheer volume meant we could now offer other retailers a price lower than they could get buying direct from the manufacturers and still make a significant profit. They saved money, we made money, and our third level of distribution—wholesaling—was in place.

After we began wholesaling, we eventually got into franchising, and ultimately franchised nine stores before we sold the whole retail operation. So our fourth level of distribution was franchising.

The point to remember is this: it's the same basketball, whether you're selling one at retail, fifty at wholesale, three thousand to an institution, or stocking your own franchises. It's the same basketball, and each sale makes a profit for you. The key is to take that basketball and sell it to as many different categories of customers as you possibly can, as efficiently as you possibly can.

This principle applies no matter what you're selling. The DoveBar most of us recognize today as ice cream on a stick thickly coated with rich chocolate got its start back in the 1950s when Leo Stefanos, who owned Dove's Candy & Ice Cream Shop in Burr Ridge, Illinois, created an irresistible treat to stop his children from chasing the Good Humor truck every day. News of the delicious confection spread, and people began asking for Dove's Bar. But sales were limited to the neighborhood store.

The children grew up and decided to package the DoveBar and sell it to supermarkets. So, in addition to a retail operation, they were also distributing wholesale. The problem was that supermarkets are not a particularly effective method of delivery for a high-end, premium product like DoveBars. They just put all the ice cream together and take their profit from whatever sells. That's okay for the supermarkets, but it wasn't exactly what the people at DoveBar had in mind.

They decided to try a third level of distribution—specialized wholesaling. They approached independent grocery stores, the Mom and Pop operations, and proposed a special DoveBar promotion. The provided displays and posters, and made a big deal out of their product. Sales skyrocketed, and everyone was making money.

DoveBar then added a fourth level of distribution: independent distributors operating DoveBar carts. Each cart had a marked umbrella and an operator wearing a DoveBar uniform, and you saw them in major airports and even in some downtown business districts across the country. It was the same ice cream confection being sold on four levels of distribution. (Today, DoveBar is expanding their product line into candy and other treats and appears to be focusing largely on grocery store distribution.)

Gardener's Supply is a leading mail-order garden equipment company, but they also have a retail store in Burlington, Vermont. A few years ago, when you thought of Sharper Image, you thought of their catalog. Now you might also think of their retail stores, which are opening up around the country. Amway, a leader in multilevel marketing, has an extensive catalog. IBM sells their products both direct to the end user and through a variety of distributor relationships. Those distributors in turn may be independent or franchises; they may sell retail, through a broker, or through a catalog.

By employing more than one level of distribution, these companies have all broadened the number of potential customers they routinely reach.

If you are in a retail business, you may opt to expand your customer base by opening another store. Certainly there are thousands of companies that have done very well by duplicating themselves. However, I suggest you approach this idea with caution. A second store may have the potential to bring in an equal amount of revenue, but it will also generate an equal amount of expense. Instead of opening a second store, if you add another method of distribution to your current operation, you can increase your revenue without significantly increasing your expenses. That's called add-on revenue, and we will discuss it in more detail in Chapter Twelve. In the meantime, remember that multiple levels of distribution translate into additional profitability.

Delivery Systems

The other half of fulfillment services is delivery—the physical method you will use to get goods or services to your customers. Just as with distribution, you have a variety of options. Your first consideration, of course, is to find a system or systems appropriate for your product. Also, you'll want to reevaluate your distribution system periodically, since additional choices may become available as technological advances are made.

Cash and Carry. Far and away the most simple type of distribution, cash and carry is usually seen in a retail situation. The process is simple: the customer brings in the cash and carries out the merchandise. Remember that cash in this case includes certain types of credit. You may want to accept certain bank credit cards or have your own internal credit program. Regardless of which payment methods you choose to accept, the concept is the same. The customer comes to you, makes a selection, pays for it, and leaves with that product. Department stores, specialty shops, and supermarkets are all examples of cash and carry. Even some mobile businesses are cash and carry.

Your business doesn't have to be retail to the public to be cash and carry. Wholesale operations like Price Costco and Sam's Wholesale Club are also cash and carry, even though their customer base is limited to qualified members. The point to remember is that retail and whole-sale are distribution systems; cash and carry is a delivery method.

On-Premise Consumption. Just because you are in a retail location doesn't mean you offer cash and carry delivery. Restaurants use a retail distribution system, but their products are consumed on the premises. Of course, smart restaurateurs will consider expanding their revenues by offering certain menu items for sale with cash and carry delivery, but we'll talk more about that later. Other types of businesses that deliver by on-premise consumption include medical services, health spas, educational programs, hairdressers, theaters, video arcades, and sporting events.

Home Delivery. Add an extra measure of convenience to the cash-and-carry system by providing delivery to your customer's home or business. You may want to do it yourself in a company-owned vehicle, or you might opt to use a local delivery service, a package service such as United Parcel Service, an airfreight company, or a common carrier. Your decision will, of course, depend on your product and the level of service required.

By offering delivery, you could eliminate the need for your customers to visit your premises, which in turn eliminates the need for an office or showroom and reduces your overhead. A delivery truck has helped many a young company operate successfully for years from the owner's garage, keeping overhead low while building a customer base.

Mail Delivery. Similar to a local delivery system, mail order has traditionally been associated with catalog sales. However, you are not limited to using the United States Postal Service; you can use United Parcel Service or any other package carrier that meets your cost and service requirements.

Common Carrier. For items too large for a package service, you need a trucking company. You may opt for an independent trucker, but you're probably safer using a recognized common carrier, such as Yellow Freight System, Consolidated Freightways, Overnite Transportation Company, and Carolina Freight Carriers. Check your telephone directory for the trucking companies serving your city. But remember, not all truckers are equal. Not every carrier goes everywhere, and the rates will vary. Many small regional carriers offer excellent service and competitive prices, while others use shabby equipment and are generally unreliable. Be sure you select a financially sound company with a good reputation; if you have a claim, you want to know they'll be around to pay it.

Air Freight. When your products are extremely time-sensitive and you need delivery across the country in hours instead of days, you will likely turn to air freight. You need to shop for an air freight company because, as in trucking, there is a wide disparity in pricing and service. Industry pioneers like Emery Worldwide will handle just about anything, while Federal Express limits package size and weight. Another consideration with air freight is commodity restrictions. Certain materials, such as flammable, corrosive, and magnetized substances, are considered hazardous on board an aircraft.

Air freight is generally the most expensive method of transportation; the charges need to be either added on or built into your price.

Drop-Shipping. I used this term when I described our agreement with Penn Athletic and the order for basketballs from the Dade County school board. It means that your supplier, whether it is the manufacturer or a wholesaler, ships the product directly to your customer. All you do is the paperwork; you never actually handle the merchandise. You don't have to worry about warehousing, packaging, or dealing with freight companies.

When you set up a drop-shipping arrangement, include the requirement that your company name and address appear on the label so your customer doesn't get the erroneous idea that they can get a better deal bypassing you and going straight to your source.

Electronic or Telephone Delivery. If your product is information, it may lend itself to delivery via a telecommunications system. Modems allow your computer to communicate with other computers, and facsimile machines mean documents can be transmitted around the world in minutes. On-line data bases, such as The Source, Genie, Prodigy, and CompuServe, which you access with your own personal computer and a modem, continue to grow in popularity and variety. Some brokers, like Charles Schwab & Co., allow you to sell and purchase stocks via modem. And as busy people opt for fewer face-to-face meetings, professionals such as attorneys, accountants, and other consultants deliver their advice on the phone and charge for the call.

Let Your Delivery Be Your Product

Just as distribution systems are "mix and match," so are delivery systems. Be creative so your delivery process has value in itself.

Earlier I made reference to mobile veterinary services. Most people don't realize this, but the veterinary business is highly competitive and very few vets will get rich from their practice. Also, starting a veterinary clinic requires a significant amount of capital—there's a building, furnishing, medical equipment, supplies, staff, and so on. But here's an alternative for vets who want their own practice but don't have the money or aren't willing to go into debt for their own clinic: buy a van, stock it with pharmaceuticals and other veterinary care products purchased on credit, have some business cards and flyers printed, and arrange for a cellular phone with voice mail. That's all it takes for a licensed vet to go into a mobile business making house calls.

Now, think about what fun it is to take your pet to the vet. You have to interrupt your business day to go home, get your pet, let it shed (or worse, if it's sick) all over your car, and take it to the animal hospital, where the unfamiliar location and clinical atmosphere make even a routine exam a traumatic experience for the animal.

Contrast that with a veterinarian who comes to you in a van equipped with all the supplies necessary to conduct the equivalent of an office visit. The dog gets examined on his own favorite pillow instead of a metal table, his stress level is significantly reduced, your car doesn't need cleaning—I think the advantages are clear.

What's more, mobile vet prices can be competitive with standing clinics because their overhead is much lower.

It's important that you not assume or take for granted anything about the delivery system for your business. Most veterinary school graduates assume they have two choices, which are both on-premise-consumption delivery systems: they can start their own standing clinic, which is an extremely expensive proposition, or they can go to work for someone else, which has no appeal to the individual with an entrepreneurial spirit. But as you've seen, they have a third choice: to start a mobile veterinary service providing home delivery. The investment is nominal and the rewards are significant.

Whether you think Domino's Pizza is the best pizza on the market is a matter of personal taste, but the company's success has been built on a home delivery concept that has spawned a host of imitators. In the case of most food delivery companies, the primary value to the consumer is the convenience of not having to go to a restaurant, stand in line to place and pick up an order, and then bring it home. The primary value is the delivery system—something Pizza Hut has also learned.

Harriet McNear combines on-premise consumption, delivery, and cash and carry in her whole foods cooking school. She holds classes in a spacious teaching kitchen in her home (keeping her overhead low); she takes her show "on the road" by teaching classes and doing consulting work in other locations; and she also sells a selection of books and utensils related to whole foods preparation and health.

Since computers have become standard equipment in most offices and an increasing number of homes, PCs have become a delivery system of their own. You can use your personal computer to order stock transactions or to conduct research in an on-line data base. If your product is time-sensitive information, you used to have to send it out via special delivery or an express service. Now you simply assign your customers an access code, and they can download the information from your computer into theirs at their own convenience. What's more, they can get the information just minutes after you've inputted it into your system, instead of waiting hours or overnight for a courier.

Certainly you should look at whatever the traditional delivery method of products similar to yours has been, but don't limit yourself to that. Consider what your product is and where your prospective customer bases are located, then use your imagination to develop effective delivery systems.

In one of my seminars, two very dynamic young women announced their intention of opening a retail store in Detroit that would specialize in clothing designed for gospel singers. Apparently, gospel singers are abundant in Detroit, and it seems that a large percentage of them are, well, abundant in more ways than one.

These two women had found a line of clothing that was perfect for gospel singers. It seemed that they had found their market niche, but I was concerned about their proposed distribution system being retail and their delivery system being cash and carry. So I asked what percentage of the nation's gospel singers lived in Detroit. They weren't sure, but guessed maybe 5 or 10 percent.

I suggested they look at ways to reach a broader base of customers more efficiently. Where are gospel singers? They are wherever there are churches. That includes not only Detroit, but Memphis, Chattanooga, Dallas, Houston, Orlando, and just about everywhere else. So why invest in a retail outlet in Detroit, which would seriously limit their customer base?

Match Your Delivery System with Your Customer Base

A more profitable arrangement for a business specializing in clothing for gospel singers would be to track major gospel events and national conventions, attend them with catalogs and samples, take orders, and then either ship from existing stock or have the manufacturer drop-ship the merchandise. Another option for these two women would be to set up distributorships, perhaps making gospel group coaches or church music directors their representatives. The distributors would receive a commission on their orders, and the clothing would be shipped from a centralized location.

Would a retail store targeted to gospel singers in Detroit have been successful? Maybe. Would a national distribution and delivery system featuring garments for gospel singers have a better chance of success? Definitely—and probably at less cost to set up.

Always be on the lookout for ways to maximize the efficiency of getting your product to the marketplace. And never, never assume you have to do it the way it's always been done, or the way everybody else does it. In most businesses, designing your fulfillment services allows you almost as much creativity as your initial product development.

Chapter Nine Highlights

—Fulfillment services basically consist of distribution and delivery.

—Distribution is the way your products get to different markets.

—Distribution systems include retail, franchise, multilevel marketing, catalog, distributorships, jobbers, wholesalers, brokers, and more.

—The more distribution levels you create, the larger number of different markets you can reach.

—Delivery is the way products are physically moved to the ultimate consumer.

—Delivery systems include cash and carry, on-premise consumption, home delivery, mail delivery, common carrier, airfreight, dropshipping, electronic or telephone, and others—and sometimes the delivery system becomes the product.

—Regularly reevaluate your delivery systems for maximum efficiency and customer satisfaction.

CHAPTER TEN

Production
Creating Profit from Value

"If you have built castles in the air your work need not be lost; that is where they should be. Now put foundations under them."

—Henry David Thoreau

WE'VE TALKED ABOUT MARKETING and fulfillment services. Now it's time to take a look at the third leg of your business, which is production. Someone has to make whatever you plan to sell.

There are three elements to this particular component of your business. First, you must set up the actual production system. Second, understand your value-added considerations. Third, develop a quality assurance program.

Your Production System

There are two ways to handle production: you can do it yourself, or you can get someone else to do it for you. Both can be profitable, and the method you choose will be based on your specific product or service.

In the case of most intangible products, such as services, the decision is fairly simple: you, or someone you hire, provides the service to your customer. In the case of a product, you have a lot of other things to consider.

When it comes to producing a tangible product, there are three primary approaches you can take: (1) manufacture the item yourself from raw materials, (2) buy an existing item and make some modifications to it, or (3) subcontract the entire manufacturing process.

Choose the approach most appropriate for your business. If your product is high-end custom clothing, you will need to manufacture each garment to your customers' specifications. But if your business is a customized T-shirt shop, you don't need to sew your own shirts. You buy the shirts and add value with airbrushing or heat-transfers. For a simple retail clothing store, you just buy the garments from the manufacturers and sell them to your customers.

Your decision should be based largely on what the value of your product is to the ultimate consumer and how you can most efficiently and economically create that value. In some cases, the value created by a product comes not from the item itself, but from the way it is sold. Or the value may come from one of the many differences we discussed in Chapter Six.

Also, keep the principles of downsizing in mind as you approach the production issue. Manufacturing increases your initial capital investment and your ongoing fixed expenses. It reduces your flexibility and makes it more difficult for you to change with your market. On the other hand, you may have a product so unique that no one else can make it for you.

But especially if the "difference that makes you different" is not in your actual product, I suggest you subcontract as much as possible. Now is not the time to reinvent the wheel. There is absolutely no reason why you should devise a way to manufacture something someone else is already making. By subcontracting as much as possible, you reduce fixed costs, and, ultimately, your financial risk.

You're in good company when you use subcontractors. Some of the largest corporations in the world have found this to be an efficient production method. Customers make their purchases based on the most appealing marketing program; they don't really care who actually assembled all the nuts and bolts. Consequently, many competing companies buy their products from the same manufacturer—the only difference is the label. Why should you try to change a system that works so well?

Does Sears manufacture Kenmore appliances? Of course not. They subcontract the work to appropriate appliance manufacturers. "Kenmore" is nothing more than the marketing label.

There are only a handful of companies that actually manufacture video cassette recorders, but the list of brand names at your nearby electronics store is plentiful. The situation is similar when it comes to photocopiers. A handful of manufacturers are building machines that are ultimately sold under a variety of labels. Ricoh makes their own copiers, as well as those marketed under the Savin and Pitney Bowes label. Toshiba manufactures copiers for 3M. Mita and TA Adler are the same machine, and the list goes on.

In my sporting goods business, we carried several different brands of baseballs. Our customers' buying decisions were based on a variety of things: price, manufacturer's reputation, performance, style, and so on. But you can't manufacture baseballs by machine; they are one of the few things left in our world that must be made by hand. The core of the ball is manually inserted into the leather pouch and then hand-stitched.

So while the baseballs we sold carried different brand names and varied performance claims, they were all assembled at the same plant in Haiti. It didn't matter who the label said the manufacturer was, they all came from this single plant on a little Caribbean island where I personally saw hundreds of Haitians spending their days stuffing baseball cores into leather pouches, sewing them shut, and then stamping the appropriate manufacturer's name on the ball. Had I wanted to, I could have easily had my own line of baseballs assembled at this plant according to my specifications. I don't have to physically produce baseballs to become a baseball manufacturer.

Virtually every wood baseball and softball bat in this country is manufactured by Hillerick & Bradsby. It doesn't matter that the specifications might be slightly different on each model, or that the names on the bats are Wilson, Spalding, Rawlings, or something else—they are all made by H & B. The same is true for aluminum bats, but the manufacturer there is Easton.

When my friend Tom got his idea for a remote headset for hearing-impaired people to use while watching television, he went to an electronics manufacturer, who then actually produced the item. Tom didn't want a production business; he wanted a business that would help the hearing-impaired.

The nature of your business may require that you do a partial amount of production. My law firm produces legal services; we don't buy those services from another law firm. Softlab produced computer software; they didn't buy programs from other companies. General Motors produces cars; they certainly don't buy them from Ford. But even so, a major portion of these operations can be subcontracted. In fact, many of the items in General Motors' cars are produced by the same companies that produce them for Ford, Chrysler, and other automobile manufacturers.

You are probably comfortable with the idea of retaining a lawyer, an accountant, even an advertising firm to handle the administrative and operating portions of your company. Extend that comfort zone to include acquiring the services of a manufacturing concern to make as much as possible of the product you plan to sell. If your market niche is the *sale* of goods and services, don't get tangled up in manufacturing them.

Obviously, there is a role for real production in the business/marketing cycle. Somebody, somewhere has to make what gets sold. When I teach a seminar, I don't subcontract that out. But I do subcontract the audio/visual experts who make and duplicate the tapes I sell. When I developed *The Desktop Lawyer,* I did the production work of creating the documents, writing the instructions, and explaining the program on an audio tape. I used subcontractors for the printing, binding, recording, duplication, and creating the computer program that would allow the product to be sold on disks. So, though you may have to do some production yourself, make sure the production you are doing is consistent with your business mission statement and with your company's function.

Consider Your Value-Added

Business production is 100 percent processing. It is processing that adds the value to your product that makes it different, and it is the value-added that people want to buy. In Chapter Six, we talked about what makes you different. Value-added is to production what difference is to marketing. And you will price according to your value-added (we'll discuss pricing more fully in Chapter Twelve).

What your raw materials are and what your finished goods turn out to be are, by and large, irrelevant. What's important is the extent to which you process and the extent to which that processing adds value.

Regardless of whether you originate or subcontract your product, there are certain steps required in production. The raw materials come in, are processed, then go out in the form of finished goods or services. No matter what your product is, the basic production steps are the same. The company that reproduces my seminar tapes takes blank tapes (the raw materials), adds my voice to the tape and a label to the cartridge (processing), and ships them (as finished goods) to me. The processing is the value-added.

Sometimes what a company produces turns out to be a raw material for someone else. Audio tapes, for example, are a raw material for my production company, but a finished product for the company that took plastic cases and magnetic tape and created a blank audio cassette. The assembly of the tape is the value-added, and it is the value-added that sells.

Restaurants are a great example of value-added. Even allowing for the fact that some recipes are more complicated than others, you can make at home just about anything you can order in a restaurant. You generally don't go to a restaurant for basic food and nourishment; you go for the service, for the ambience, for the convenience—you go for the value the restaurant adds to the food.

Classes at Harriet's Kitchen don't teach anything you can't find in a book, but the value-added is that you don't have to take the time to read the books, plus you have the personal interaction with a teacher. You can buy a computer from a lot of places, even by mail order, but the value-added from a retail computer store is personal service and a sincere concern for customer satisfaction.

It works the same way when your product is information. You can take raw data, compile it, process it, and turn out a finished product in the form of a book, magazine, newsletter—or even a seminar.

Labor works the same way. Take an untrained individual, provide education, and your finished product is expert labor. That labor may be in the form of a doctor, a physicist, a business consultant, a secretary, or any type of skill in demand by the marketplace.

The key to the value of your product is in the processing, whether you do it yourself or arrange to have it done. The value you add to the raw materials by processing them is what you communicate in your marketing process.

What is the value-added of your product or service? If you don't know, you're not ready to start your business.

THE PRODUCTION PROCESS

Raw Materials	+	Processing (Value-Added)	=	Finished Product

Parts	Equipment	Assembled goods
Components	Technology	Inventory
Random information	Analysis and tabulation	Refined information
Personnel	Education	Skilled labor
Intrinsic materials	Programming	Merchandise
Sub-parts	Packaging	Parts
Sub-components	Assembly	Components
Electronics	Compilation	Energy
Your raw materials	Your processing	Your finished product

Processing is the value-added of your finished product.

Production Can Be a Global Issue

A large percentage of production facilities are located overseas. If you've never done business in the international marketplace, don't let that intimidate you. The world has indeed become a global village, and foreign concerns are eager to do business with American companies, large or small. And if you're worried about being too small, remember we don't have a monopoly on small businesses, and there is absolutely no reason to assume international trade is limited to corporate giants. It's not.

Think about this: There is a whole section of the world—Eastern Europe and the countries of the former Soviet Union—beginning once again to get their feet wet in business, and they're looking for you.

The U. S. Department of Commerce is a good place to start if you need help learning the mechanics of doing business on a worldwide scale. In the international marketplace, a good import broker and a freight forwarder are as important as your attorney and accountant are at home. The import broker will handle processing the materials you bring in from other countries through customs; the freight forwarder handles what you export. Choose qualified, experienced agents to handle these tasks, because the errors in the paperwork can cause delays at the least, and may be responsible for higher duties and even fines. Local organizations, such as a community college, the chamber of commerce, and other professional groups, usually offer educational assistance to companies who want to expand internationally.

So how do you find the manufacturers who make what you need? On an international level, start with the *Directory of International Concerns* produced by the Chamber of Commerce. Within the United States, check the *Thomas Registry*. Both directories are available in most libraries.

Whether you buy domestically or internationally, and whether you buy raw materials and do extensive processing or buy a finished product from a subcontractor, production, simply put, means establishing what you are going to do. It's your value-added.

Once you've determined what your value-added will be, you need to consider quality. Quality became a corporate buzzword during the 1980s for a good reason: it's an essential ingredient for success.

Your Quality Assurance Program

It's natural to be concerned about the quality of subcontracted products, but remember most subs are as concerned about maintaining their customer base as you are. You are the customer. They must keep you happy or you'll buy from someone else. A business owner who consistently allows shipments of sloppy products, with the attitude that it doesn't matter because the ultimate consumer is not their customer, is someone who won't be a business owner very long.

As an extra measure of quality assurance, insert a clause in your subcontractor agreement that the price of any defective merchandise will be refunded. If someone buys a copy of *The Desktop Lawyer* and finds a page missing, I don't pay the printer for that copy.

If someone buys a set of six or eight seminar tapes and finds that one tape consistently jams in the player, I don't pay the subcontractor for that entire set of tapes. Now, I only have to provide my customer with the missing page or one defective tape, but I also have to take the time to smooth over a rough situation, to provide customer service. So I feel this approach to vendors is justified.

When you negotiate with subcontractors, be sure to cover all your bases, including payment terms and delivery dates. If your sub has to make a significant investment in materials up front, it's not unreasonable to expect to have to pay a deposit. What's important is having a clear, mutually agreeable payment schedule.

The delivery date is also critical. If your own delivery method is mail order, you may opt to withhold your product order until you see what type of response you get from a specific promotion. The efficiency is obvious: you only buy what you know you can sell. But you have a moral and legal obligation to provide delivery within a reasonable period of time, so you must have a subcontractor that can meet your delivery commitment.

I know from experience that when I teach a wealth-building seminar, approximately a third of the participants will want to buy *The Desktop Lawyer*. My seminars are scheduled several months in advance, and I usually have a pretty good idea how many people will be attending. So I make sure I have enough copies in the back of the room to make those sales right then and there.

The Desktop Lawyer includes a book, a set of audio tapes, and a set of computer disks, and I know how long it takes to produce each component. My vendors get ample notice, and they know I expect them to meet their delivery date—or suffer the consequences outlined in the penalty clause in our contract. But I don't want to have to take advantage of a penalty clause; no penalty clause is going to compensate me for lost sales and lost customer goodwill. I want a reliable subcontractor who will meet their delivery commitment every time.

So I'm going to remind you of a very basic business operating principle: check references.

Checking references is an elementary practice that could literally save your business. You wouldn't—or at least, you shouldn't—hire an employee without doing a background investigation, and applicants expect to provide references.

Subcontractors are no different. These vendors are your "employees" on a much larger scale, and you have a right to know as much about them as you do about anyone on your payroll. Don't assume that any reference they give you will necessarily be a good one. Call each one anyway. Ask questions like the following: How long have they been using the vendor in question? (If every reference is a short-term customer but the vendor claims to have been in business for twenty years, that should make you suspicious.) How is the quality of the product? How does the vendor handle problems? Has the reference used other vendors of this type, and how does this one compare? Do they plan to continue using the vendor long-term? Why or why not? What is the reference's volume and how does it compare to yours?

If you are going to be doing any of the production work yourself, set up an internal system of checks and balances so nothing but the highest quality goes out the door. That could mean a visual inspection of the merchandise, or a second person checking the count, or whatever quality-control method is appropriate for your product. If a mistake should slip by, your customer service program (which we discussed in Chapter Six), should include a plan for handling problems.

Understand that you cannot eliminate production, no matter what business you are in. But just because you are in business doesn't mean you necessarily have to produce anything. Your "production" may actually be minor processing, or a unique delivery system, or a special marketing plan. Whatever it involves, the production leg of your business must be as strong as the marketing and fulfillment legs. Once in place, it will not demand as much of your attention, but it must be a consistently performing component of your company.

So examine all your options before you start, and then review them on a regular basis to make sure you continue to use the method that is best for you.

Now that we have examined the three major aspects of your business—marketing, fulfillment services, and production—it's time to add the glue that holds the whole structure together: operations.

Chapter Ten Highlights

—There are three legs to the production aspect of your business: the actual production system; a quality assurance program; and your value-added considerations.

—Your production system can include doing production yourself internally, farming it out to subcontractors, or a combination of the two.

—Using subcontractors is usually the most efficient method of production.

—A thorough quality assurance program means satisfied customers who will buy from you again.

—Detailed subcontractor agreements are a key part of quality assurance.

—If necessary, seek out subcontractors in other countries.

—The value-added of your product or service is the value that comes from the processing you provide. The value-added is the benefit you are offering your customers, and is usually what will convince your market to buy from you.

—Though value-added is a production issue and pricing is a marketing issue, you should price according to value-added for maximum profitability.

CHAPTER ELEVEN

Operations
The Support Platform of Your Business

"Our main business is not to see what lies dimly at a distance,
but to do what lies clearly at hand."
—Thomas Carlyle,
Scottish Critic and Historian

I HAVE SAID that your business has three aspects: marketing, fulfillment, and production, which are supported on a platform known as operations. Operations is the part of your infrastructure that supports the continuation and/or expansion of your ongoing business objectives; it's the engine that drives your business.

I have also said that any business operated well can be profitable. A critical part of operating well is keeping your business as simple and streamlined as possible. Don't make things more complicated than they have to be. There's no reason to appoint a committee when one person can do the job.

Think of operations as the skeleton holding the other components of your business together. But remember, there is nothing inherently valuable about operations. Marketing earns money by communicating with customers so they are prompted to buy. Fulfillment services earn money through the distribution and delivery of your product. Production earns money by creating the product marketing sells. Operations, by contrast, never earn money, they only cost money.

Operations are only valuable to the extent that they support the three major aspects of your company: marketing, fulfillment services, and distribution. Nobody will buy something from you just because your operational structure is interesting, so don't worry about being especially creative here. Just build a solid foundation based on sound business principles, and you will come as close to failure-proofing your business as is possible.

Your operational infrastructure can be nothing more than a desk and a typewriter or personal computer in the spare bedroom of your home. It can be nothing more than a part-time clerk who answers the phone and takes orders five hours a day. Or it can be a factory, or a warehouse, or employees. Whatever it is, it is pure, unadulterated *cost.*

Operations do not produce value. The value of your business is in marketing, fulfillment, and production. Keep that in mind as you allocate resources and energy.

In operations, you have three primary concerns: your legal structure, your financial structure, and your operational structure. Let's begin by taking a look at your options when it comes to legal structure.

Legal Structure

I can't count the number of times when someone has come to me as their attorney and said, "Larry, I'm going to start a business. I need to incorporate." I believe it would be malpractice on my part simply to draw up the papers without finding out where in the business start-up process that client is. Because until you have identified your customer, until you know how you will market, distribute, and produce, you can't make the best decision regarding your legal and financial structure.

My general advice is to incorporate only when absolutely necessary. Don't assume just because you plan to run your business and carry the title of president that you must be a corporation. Or that the president of the corporation will run the business. Who runs your business is part of your operational structure, who the officers are is part of your legal structure, and the two structures are different. How your business looks and functions operationally doesn't say a thing about how it looks legally. Before you make a final decision regarding your legal structure, there are three major areas you need to consider:

Risk Reduction. Sometimes risk reduction is referred to as "limitation of liability," but that is only one facet of risk reduction. Business is inherently risky, if for no other reason than that you are ultimately going to subject yourself to the vote of the marketplace. Everyone who goes into business anticipates the acceptance of some economic risk— it goes with the territory. At the same time, it's important to eliminate or reduce as much non-economic risk as possible. Non-economic risk includes doing things that are just plain dumb, like exposing yourself to more liability than you have to, either by your conduct or your legal structure.

Ease of Operation. If you really wanted me to, I could create a legal structure that I guarantee would protect all of your assets for the rest of your life. Of course, it would be so cumbersome and so difficult for you to operate that it would take a major international transaction for you to go to the grocery store and buy a pound of coffee. Everything in life has its trade-offs, and this is one of them. Your legal structure is in place to support your business, not to weigh it down, so make sure it is one that will allow you the flexibility to operate and grow without undue difficulties. From both an operational and a legal stand-point, your structure needs to provide internal integrity and allow each component to operate both independently and interdependently with the others.

Asset Protection. As your business grows and you accumulate assets, you want to be sure that they are subject to as little risk as possible. Some assets can be protected by your legal structure; others require insurance; and there are certain circumstances when you will be vulnerable no matter what you do.

When You Should Incorporate

There are four sets of circumstances under which you would be wise to incorporate in order to limit your liability. But first, let me point out that you cannot totally eliminate liability. A corporation will not limit your liability with respect to a secured creditor. If someone has loaned the corporation money using a piece of your equipment as collateral and you default on the loan, they'll come get the equipment. Period. What they can't do is get a personal judgment against you.

A corporation also doesn't protect you against institutional creditors, because I don't know of any bank that will make a loan to a small business corporation without a personal guarantee.

Third, a corporation will not protect you against casualty or hazard liability. What protects you there is insurance, and I'll talk about that in more detail later.

Finally, a corporation will not protect you against the Internal Revenue Service. You cannot bankrupt yourself out of taxes; you don't even get out of paying taxes when you die. There is no escaping the IRS. They will attach your personal assets, they will attach your estate— they *will* get their money.

What a corporation will protect you against is unsecured creditor liability—the first set of circumstances under which you should consider incorporating. Unsecured creditor liability is what you owe that is not backed up with collateral of any sort; if you default, there is no specific item the creditor can repossess. If you own a restaurant, you probably buy your food from several different vendors, and unless you're on C.O.D. terms with all of them, you'll have unsecured creditor liability. If you're in a retail store, your merchandise vendors are unsecured creditors. Your corporation will protect your personal assets if something happens and you cannot pay these vendors.

The second condition under which you should incorporate is if you are in a high-risk business. If there is a strong rate of injury or death related directly to your business, incorporate and have the corporation buy plenty of insurance. A construction company is an excellent example of a high-risk business, because you have no idea what your next source of liability will be. You might build a house and the electrical subcontractor does a lousy wiring job and the house catches fire and burns down. Trust me, if that happens, you'll get sued. Or if some overly curious youngster wanders onto one of your construction sites, trips over a board, and gets hurt, it doesn't matter that the kid was trespassing, you'll get sued. So even if you don't have unsecured creditor liability, if you are in a high-risk business, go ahead and incorporate.

Corporations can also be effective when you are exposed to substantial contingent or contractual liability. When you expose yourself to promises, contracts, or commitments to do something and you fail or default on those commitments, your liability may result in consequential damages against you. A consequential damage is the damage caused another person as a consequence of your breach or action. The amount of consequential damages is not measured by how much money was at stake in your agreement, but by how much money that person lost as a result of what you did or didn't do.

To illustrate this, let's say your contract called for the delivery of five thousand Christmas widgets by November 20, for which you were charging $1 each. Because of your policy on seasonal items, your customer, a retail store, paid you in advance. But you ran into some problems and couldn't fill the order until January 10. The store had planned to sell the Christmas widgets at $5 each. They would likely sue you, not only for the $5,000 they paid for the merchandise, but for the $20,000 that is the total of their lost profit. These are consequential damages. So when you will be exposing yourself to contract or contingent liability, it's best to incorporate.

The final category of businesses that should be incorporated are those with a high fatality rate. For example, restaurants have a notoriously high fatality rate. They can operate successfully for twenty years and be out of business in three weeks. That's because restaurants are not like stores, which can build inventory and have a cushion against a bad season. A restaurant's inventory is the hundreds of dollars' worth of meat, fish, and vegetables in the kitchen. They can't serve you the milk they bought a few weeks ago that nobody has ordered yet. Restaurants are a cash in, cash out business, and just a few bad weeks can force them into bankruptcy. As is commonly said, a restaurant is only as good as its last meal.

Of course, you don't go into any business thinking you'll fail, just as you don't get married thinking you'll get divorced. But just as more and more people are entering into prenuptial agreements, if your business is one with a high fatality rate, you should go ahead and incorporate. If you don't need the protection of the corporate structure, that's great; but if you do, it's there.

When a Corporation Won't Protect You

A corporation is a separate and distinct legal entity that must remain separate and distinct to serve its purpose. Even though you may be the president and sole shareholder, you must preserve the separateness of your corporation, or you may find yourself in an uncomfortably vulnerable position.

If you formed your corporation to reduce risk and protect your assets, you want to make sure, in the event of a lawsuit, that your legal structure will stand up in court. You know from reading the papers that when people sue these days, they sue the corporation, they sue the individuals involved, and they sue anybody else they can find with enough assets to make it worth their while—and even people who don't have any assets. Now, to get to your personal assets, the plaintiff must prove you either had personal liability or—and this is what happens most of the time—their lawyer has to prove that your corporation was not operated as a separate and distinct legal entity. That's called piercing the corporate veil, and attorneys can do it three ways.

First, when the corporation starts paying your personal expenses, you are opening the door to problems. Processing your business and personal funds through the same account is called commingling, and it can get you into a lot of trouble. So don't buy groceries or make your mortgage payment from the corporate bank account. Pay yourself a salary from the corporation, deposit it into a personal account, and handle your own non-business expenses from your personal accounts. That sounds so simple, but it's been my experience as a commercial litigator that at least three-fourths of the time, people do not operate their corporations as if they were separate entities. And the degree to which I can show commingling of corporate and personal resources is the degree to which I can hold the individual liable for the activities of the corporation.

A corporate expense is a corporate expense; a personal expense is a personal expense. Keep them separate, or you will eliminate any protection against personal liability your corporation might have provided.

There's another wrinkle here, too, and that's the Internal Revenue Service. Once you start paying personal expenses out of your corporation, you're going to give some IRS auditor a field day because you've destroyed the presumption that every check the corporation writes is for a legitimate business expense. So respect the separateness of the corporate entity, have separate bank accounts, and clearly document every financial transaction.

The second way an attorney can pierce the corporate veil is in the area of record keeping. By law, you must have a shareholders' meeting and a board of directors meeting at least once a year. Other requirements will vary from state to state. If you don't have thousands of shareholders, your annual meeting doesn't have to be a major event. But it does need to be held and minutes need to be kept. Those minutes should include a financial statement and reflect significant corporate transactions, such as loans and the sale or purchase of major assets. Don't worry about creating a literary masterpiece, just make sure you have annual records of what's going on in your corporation. You can't maintain the integrity of the corporate entity if you are not keeping proper records as required by the legal structure of your organization.

And don't think if someone sues you that you can quickly create the necessary documents and back-date them. First, it's illegal, and second, you'll probably get caught. There are always things that will give you away: different equipment (like a new word processor or typewriter), different employees, inconsistent dates. If you have trouble remembering your anniversary or your mother's birthday, you're going to have some real problems creating a set of back-dated corporate documents.

If you try to use back-dated corporate documents and you are called to give a deposition, which is done under oath, you have two choices: you can tell the truth, in which case the opposing attorney can pierce the corporate veil; or you can lie, in which case you've committed perjury—a criminal offense. When it's all over, you will have lost the case, you may be subject to criminal penalties, and your credibility will be shot. Believe me, it's much easier just to adhere from the start to the laws of your state regarding record-keeping.

Every year I send letters to all my corporate clients telling them it's time to come in and take care of their corporate documents. I let them know what they need to be prepared to discuss, we set an appointment, they come in, and the whole thing is over in about five minutes. It's a whole lot easier and less painful than going to the dentist, and it can make all the difference in the world when you get hit by a plaintiff's attorney with a notice to produce your corporate records.

The third way to pierce the corporate veil is to prove inadequate capitalization. By this I mean inadequate in relationship to the risks associated with the business to a third party or to the public. If you have a very small business that doesn't offer a lot of risks, you need less capital. Also, we're not talking about the same capital a bank might want to see when considering you for a loan. For this standard, insurance operates like capital, because the law and the courts treat the face value of an insurance policy as if it is capital belonging to the corporation. You may only have $1,000 in cash and assets in your corporation, but if you also have a $50,000 insurance policy, the law will treat you as though you had $50,000 of capital added to the assets of the company.

If you're operating a word processing service from your home, your risk of injury to the public is extremely limited and, accordingly, so is your need for insurance. But if you're manufacturing football helmets, you'd better have a substantial insurance policy, because there is no amount of capital you could possibly have in your company that would protect you after an accident when somebody argues that you were inadequately capitalized. If your business offers risks to your customers or the general public, protect yourself with a good business umbrella policy.

If you've gone to the effort of creating a corporate shell, of paying the annual filing fees (they're not much, but it's still a consideration), of setting up separate records, then invest the effort to maintain the integrity of that legal entity. Don't be foolish by being too busy to hold your annual meeting or by writing a business check for your groceries because you forgot to order your personal checks and ran out of them. Treat your corporation with respect and let it serve you.

Document Your Business Relationships

Documentation is critical in your relationships with other people, especially when it comes to items such as your stockholders agreement or your partnership agreement. Do you need a written agreement when you're going into business with someone you've known for years and trust implicitly? You most certainly do, and trust doesn't enter into it. What if you create a successful business and in twenty years your partner wants to sell it and you don't? What if your partner gets a divorce and his ex-wife gets his share of the business as part of the settlement? What if your partner dies and you wind up in business with her flaky son? Or what if your partner runs into financial difficulties and one of his creditors attaches his stock in the business?

All of these possibilities should be addressed in a stockholders or partnership agreement. It's not a question of trust, it's a question of good business practice. And such an agreement could very well save your friendship.

All of this time spent explaining corporations has led up to a repeat of my original point: don't incorporate if you don't have to. Did you notice the only time I mentioned taxes was in relation to your liability to the IRS? That's because tax benefits do not come from incorporating. The easiest way to operate and get the best tax benefits is as a sole proprietorship. As a sole proprietor, you simply file a schedule C with your personal tax return, and you are entitled to as many as twenty-nine additional deductions for ordinary and necessary expenses that have become deductible by virtue of the fact that they are expenses associated with your business.

You incorporate only when the nature of your business suggests you need the protection of a corporation to limit your liability.

What Are Your Risks?

There is nothing in this world that doesn't have some degree of risk, and some types of businesses are more risky than others. The key is to understand what your potential risks are and take steps to minimize them. Consider the worst possible case scenario of every aspect of your business, and figure out what you would need to protect yourself and the company from the consequences. This is the time for a lengthy conference with your insurance agent, who should be willing to make a personal visit to your premises to assist you in reducing physical risks and selecting the right coverage.

Property. Regardless of where your business is housed, you need to protect your property. If you own or lease a facility solely for business purposes, it should meet or exceed local safety codes. Install an alarm system. Make sure your parking lot is well lighted. Don't allow customers into potentially hazardous areas and provide as much protection as possible for your employees. Affix permanent identification marks to every piece of equipment. If your business is in your home, check with your insurance agent to see what's covered under your homeowner's policy and how much additional coverage you should buy.

Data Protection. Computers have allowed most businesses to store virtually all of their important data on disks. In the event of a data loss, most insurance companies will pay for the cost of the software but not for the cost of data recovery. And if your important records are kept on paper instead of a computer, your reimbursement will probably be limited to the actual cost of the record books. All sensitive information should be duplicated and one set of data stored in a separate physical location from your main place of business. If you have an office, keep a set of data at home. If you work at home, rent a safe deposit box for your backup data. And update those records regularly; depending on your type of business, weekly or daily backups could mean the difference between survival or failure in the event of a disaster.

Product Liability. The questions here are, how likely is it that someone could get hurt while using your product, and could your product be at fault? For most businesses, product liability is not an issue, but if you suspect that it may be in your case, consult a risk-reduction analyst to determine your best course of action.

Financial Structure

Like your legal structure, your financial structure should be kept as simple as possible while still meeting your needs. With the affordability of personal computers and the abundance of user-friendly financial software packages on the market, there is no reason why you should not have immediate access to all of the financial data affecting your company. There are a number of computer programs that will not only keep your financial records, but also track inventory, record sales, and issue statements. This means that literally in seconds you can have a complete picture of the financial status of your company.

For some reason, many owners of very small businesses feel that they do not need to concern themselves with things like profit and loss statements or asset and liability statements, but that perception is wrong. If you are seriously in business, you need to know what your financial status is, and you should examine your financial reports at least monthly. You need to be able to see the relationships among the numbers. You need economic data to back up management decisions. Without this information, you have no way of knowing if you are spending too much money in production, or if your marketing campaigns are paying off, or if there are ways you can reduce costs—all of which knowledge will naturally increase profits.

The two statements that are most critical are your profit and loss statement and your assets and liabilities statement.

Profit and Loss Statement. The profit and loss statement, commonly referred to as the P&L and sometimes as the income statement, reports what you have done in revenue and expenses, and if those activities have resulted in a net profit or loss.

The first category on your P&L is gross revenue, which is all the revenue generated by the business. This includes not just product sales, but income from interest and any other source.

The second category is cost of revenue. These are the costs specifically tied to the production of the product or service being sold. They include the cost of materials, labor, advertising and promotion, distribution, monies paid to subcontractors—anything that is directly related to revenue. For example, in a restaurant, the cost of revenue includes food, wages paid to cooks and servers, and the ad that runs in the entertainment section of the local paper promoting weekly dinner specials. These are all costs that contribute directly to revenue production.

When you subtract the second category from the first, you come up with your net revenue. Some people call this number gross profit, but I disagree. Your net revenue isn't profit at all, it's a contribution to the cost of your overhead—which leads us to the next section of your P&L: operating expenses.

As we discussed earlier, there is nothing profitable about your infrastructure. It just costs you money. So under operating expenses, you include things like rent, utilities, administrative staff salaries, repairs and maintenance, and so on—all things which do not vary based on your revenue.

Then you subtract your operating expenses from your net revenue, and finally you have your net profit or loss.

Your profit and loss statement is designed to give you a clear picture of what's coming in and what's going out. If you don't like the numbers, you can work on changing them by changing the way you operate, but you can't change the numbers until you know what they are to start with.

If yours is an average American business, out of every dollar you receive in gross revenue, 65¢ will go to the cost of revenue production and 35¢ will be your contribution to overhead. Of that 35¢, 29.5 will go to expenses, and you'll be left with a net profit of 5.5 cents. Those are national statistics, but they don't have to apply to your business. In the next two chapters, we'll take a look at a variety of ways you can reduce costs and increase revenue and profits.

SAMPLE PROFIT AND LOSS STATEMENT

Complete Industrial Products

Profit and Loss Statement

Month Ended May 31, 1991

Revenue		$15,000.00
Cost of Revenue		(9,750.00)
Inventory	$ 6,500.00	
Sales Commissions	2,750.00	
Promotional Cost	500.00	
Contribution to Overhead		5,250.00
Expenses		(4,425.00)
Rent	725.00	
Utilities	200.00	
Salaries	3,000.00	
Building Maintenance	500.00	
Net Profit for the Month		$ 825.00

Asset and Liability Statement. I call the profit and loss statement a statement of performance, because it tells you how you have been doing historically. By contrast, I call the asset and liability statement a statement of current condition, because it essentially tells you what you have and what you owe, which is the current condition of your company. This report is also known as a balance sheet.

On the asset side, you begin by listing current assets, which are cash and cash equivalents. Cash equivalents are generally receivables (what people owe you) and inventory (items you have on hand that can be sold), because they are easily converted to cash.

List your fixed assets, but understand that fixed assets, no matter how much they might have cost you, only have real value to the extent that they help you generate revenue.

What are fixed assets? For a restaurant, it's the building if you own it, the tables and chairs, the table and serviceware, and the kitchen equipment. In a retail store, it's the fixtures, gondolas, and racks that allow merchandise to be displayed. In a machine shop, it's the equipment that makes it possible to produce the product. In my law firm, it's the extensive legal library we must maintain, along with the computers, typewriters, facsimile machine, and other office equipment necessary to provide our clients with service.

Once you've listed your assets, move to the other side of the page and list your liabilities. As with assets, you have two categories of liabilities: current, which are due within the current calendar or fiscal year, and deferred, which are due subsequent to the end of the current calendar or fiscal year. For example, if you have a loan, the portion due this year is a current liability; the portion due next year is a deferred liability.

Below liabilities, list what your accountant would call owner's equity, that is, the difference between assets and liabilities. Your total assets should equal your total liabilities plus owner's equity.

Your primary concern when you look at your asset and liability statement is not whether it balances—that's a bookkeeping exercise—but the comparison of what you have versus what you owe, and how much is current in cash or cash equivalents.

These two reports are your professional report card, and they are basic and easy to prepare. Lending institutions and prospective investors will want to see them before making a decision about becoming involved with your company. More importantly, the information they contain will help you make management decisions about your business's growth and direction.

Your profit and loss statement is both valuable and essential as a business tool, because it tells you how you are doing on a day-to-day basis. Last week may have been one of the busiest weeks you've ever had, and you may have worked until midnight every night to fill all the orders, but only your profit and loss statement will tell you if you really made money during that period.

When you have your financial information clearly charted out, you can track where your money is going and make decisions on what you can do to reduce expenses and increase profits.

We'll talk more about the mechanics of functioning for cash and profit in the next chapter, but for now, understand that this simple but effective financial structure is all that is truly necessary for efficient operations.

SAMPLE ASSET AND LIABILITY STATEMENT

Complete Industrial Products

Asset and Liability Statement

December 31, 1990

Current Assets		$34,300.00
Cash	$ 3,000.00	
Accounts Receivable	1,300.00	
Inventory	30,000.00	
Fixed Assets		4,500.00
Warehouse Equipment	2,500.00	
Office Furnishings	2,000.00	
Total Assets		$38,800.00

Current Liabilities		
Accounts Payable	$ 1,500.00	
Deferred Liabilities		
Bank Loan	5,000.00	
Owner's Equity	32,300.00	
Total Liabilities and Owner's Equity		$38,800.00

Operational Structure

How you conduct the day-to-day operations of your business depends on your operational structure. It needs to be clearly defined to avoid confusion but, at the same time, flexible enough to avoid confusion but, at the same time, flexible enough to allow for growth and unexpected circumstances.

When setting up your operational structure, consider the following:

- Who is responsible for what? Titles aren't necessarily important, but even staffers in small companies should have clearly defined job descriptions to avoid friction and misunderstandings.
- Where will you operate—at home, in a commercial office, in a warehouse?
- What equipment and supplies are necessary to maintain your infrastructure, as minimal as that might be? Usually this includes office furniture and administrative materials. Will used equipment be adequate, or must you have new?
- How many employees do you need? Should they be actual employees of the company or independent contractors? Will they work in your office or at some other location?
- What type of communications equipment do you need? How many telephones and lines are necessary? Do you need a cellular phone or a pager? If your customer base extends beyond the local calling area, should you install a toll-free number? If you have a computer, should you also have a modem? Do you need a facsimile machine, and if so, how elaborate does it need to be?
- How will purchasing be handled? Who has the authority to spend money, and how much can they spend without someone else's approval? What systems will you use to assure the best value for the least price?

Learn to Communicate

One of the most important aspects of a business, and one which will quickly show the difference between an amateur and a professional businessperson, is communication. Telecommunications technology has made transmitting information over short or long distances faster and easier than ever before. Because it's so easy to pick up the phone, it's become equally easy to forget important details. Never rely solely on your memory—*write it down*. And send a copy of it to anyone affected by the conversation.

Consider this example: you're trying to entice George to invest in your business. Over the course of several months and numerous telephone conversations, you agree that George will get a 25 percent interest in the company if he invests $25,000, but if he wants to put up a lesser amount, like $20,000, he'll only get 15 percent of the company. You don't confirm anything in writing, and when George gets ready to make his investment, he writes you a check for $20,000 and expects 25 percent of the company. George probably isn't lying, and it's unlikely he's out to cheat you. The fact is, he simply doesn't remember the details.

This misunderstanding could have been prevented if, at the end of each conversation during which some issue was resolved, you had jotted down a quick note that said, "Dear George: This is to confirm our conversation today in which we indicated we are moving toward a joint venture development of the property on the corner of Main and Church streets. The points we have discussed include . . . " and then you list them. If George's perception of the conversation is different from yours, you'll be able to resolve the situation before it becomes a problem.

Every communication has two basic parts: the actual declaration and the request. The declaration states the situation; the request lets the person you're communicating with know what you want him or her to do.

In the case of the deal with George, the part of the letter mentioned above is the declaration. You include the request by closing with "If anything in this letter does not meet with your understanding, please get back to me before Friday. Best wishes."

This type of correspondence makes it clear that if George does not get back to you, it means that he has the same understanding of the situation that you do. It's a process called shifting the burden of moving forward to the other side. When you shift the burden, silence is presumed to be acquiescence.

Every significant conversation you have should be confirmed in writing. Not only does doing so prevent a possible conflict in how things are recollected, but you are creating a record that will provide you with an audit trail if it should become necessary—as when you call a supplier and tell them their latest shipment is defective, and they say they'll get back to you with disposition instructions, but they never do, and three months later they're demanding payment for the goods.

From a legal standpoint, I can't tell you how many times good documentation has allowed me to win lawsuits for my clients. On the flip side of that, poorly maintained records have created some real problems when we've tried to prove what really happened in a conflict.

When I first got into business, I had to force myself to sit down at a typewriter—we didn't have word processors or personal computers then—and bang out my "this will confirm our conversation" letters. Today I use a dictating unit, and I have a secretary who transcribes my correspondence. If you don't want to type letters yourself and hiring an employee isn't practical, find a secretarial service to do it for you. But the bottom line is, get it done.

I stress documentation because the plain truth is entrepreneurs are awful at it. They're happiest dealing with product development, marketing, or selling. They're miserable dealing with day-to-day administration. But all too often businesses suffer because some preventable oversight occurred in this area and compounded itself into an insurmountable problem.

Of course, that's not going to happen to you, because you know better. And now that you know how to set up your business, it's time to look at ways to increase your profitability.

Chapter Eleven Highlights

—Operations are the support platform of your business.

—There is nothing inherently valuable about operations; they are a pure expense.

—Incorporate your business only when necessary. Most of the time, a sole proprietor structure is adequate.

—Incorporating *will not* limit your liability with respect to a secured creditor; it will not protect you against institutional creditors; it will not protect you against casualty or hazard liability; and it will not protect you from the IRS.

—Incorporating *will* protect you against unsecured creditor liability; if you are in a high-risk business; if you are exposed to substantial contingent or contractual liability; or if your business has a high fatality rate.

—Respect the integrity of your corporation by not commingling corporate and personal resources, by maintaining proper records, and by adequate capitalization.

—Document all of your business relationships.

—Keep your financial structure simple. The two most important reports you should examine regularly are your profit and loss statement and your assets and liabilities statement.

—Take steps to reduce risk in all aspects of your business.

—Set up a clear structure for the day-to-day operation of your business.

—Follow up all verbal communications with a written confirmation of content and understanding.

CHAPTER TWELVE

Functional Processing
Functioning for Profit and Cash

"The worst crime against working people is a company which fails to operate at a profit."

—Samuel Gompers, first President of the
American Federation of Labor (AFL)

WHEN YOU WERE GROWING UP, you probably played a game that went something like this: one child would say a word, the next would repeat that word and add another, the next would repeat the first two words and add another, and so on until someone forgot one of the words and then that youngster was "out." You might feel a little as if we're playing that game here, as I tell you that even though you have found your market niche, decided on a marketing program, established distribution and delivery systems, determined your product or service and how you will produce it, and created an operational infrastructure, you can't kick back and relax—at least, not yet.

Every business can make a profit if it is operated correctly, and you now have the tools to do that. But you need not stop with a simple profit. There are specific things you can do to insure and maximize that profit, and that's what I call functional processing.

You have a solid basis on which to build your company, but the extent of your success depends on how you perform now that you are up and running. Functional processing is a procedure for identifying, clarifying, and mastering those aspects of your business that are essential to the efficient and appropriate functioning of your operation.

The three areas vital to a successful operation are profitability, cash management, and human resource development.

Functioning for Profitability

Some people have been known to get so wrapped up in what they are doing, they lose sight of the issue of profitability. Always remember that in business, you must make a profit. Your business mission statement may be to assist the hearing-impaired, or to provide a treatment facility for anorexic girls, or to produce environmentally safe products, but the natural by-product of that business is the profit it produces. If you're not producing a profit, you're not operating well. And if you aren't making a profit, you won't be in business for long. You must function for profitability, and you begin with an effective cost control system.

Cost Containment

Before we take a look at the particulars of the system, I'd like to remind you that you have only two types of costs: those related to revenue (cost of revenue) and those related to infrastructure (expenses). As we discussed in the previous chapter, revenue expenses are directly associated with marketing, selling, or making your product or service. Infrastructure costs are the things you will pay every month—such as rent, utilities, taxes, salaries, and so on—whether or not you are selling anything. Revenue expenses are variable; they will adjust with your sales. Infrastructure costs are fixed; it doesn't matter how much or how little you sell, they stay approximately the same.

There are a number of issues involved in cost containment. They include zero-based budgeting, converting fixed expenses into variable expenses, and applying the tests of essentiality and efficiency. Let's take them one at a time.

Zero-Based Budgeting. As its name implies, zero-based budgeting starts with zero and moves up from there. It doesn't start with a cost and move down. I say this because there are so many things you can do to advance your business that require no financial outlay at all.

When I first started my law practice, I issued media releases and held press conferences every time I filed a lawsuit. I received great media coverage, and I didn't pay a dime for it. I couldn't have bought that type of coverage if I had been so inclined, because first, it was news coverage, not advertising; second, to advertise as a lawyer would not have attracted the corporate market I was targeting; and third, I didn't have the money to pay for advertising anyway.

When you want something, start with zero and move up. It's like bargaining for a pair of earrings in Acapulco. Ask the shopkeeper how much they cost, he'll tell you twenty-five dollars. So you offer him a dollar. He counters by dropping the price to eighteen. You come up to two dollars. He comes down to fourteen. And so it goes until you both hit the same number.

So whatever it is that you want, assume you can get it for nothing. How much do you want to pay? That's a stupid question. You want to pay zero, of course, because you're operating on zero-based budgeting. Approach price negotiations with this attitude, and the price you end up paying will always be less than if you assign a dollar value ahead of time.

Converting Fixed Expenses into Variable Expenses. Since variable expenses are directly related to your revenue and will rise and fall with your sales revenue, it makes sense to convert as many of your expenses as possible to revenue expenses. And it always amazes me how many business owners do the exact opposite.

When I first met Chuck Givens, he had a staff of less than a dozen people. He toured the country putting on what's known in the seminar business as lead lectures—that is, free sessions designed to sell you his complete program, which consisted of a two-day live seminar and a manual and cassette tape package you could take home. He lectured in the front of the room, and his staff was in the back selling the product. Ideally, he wanted people always to be able to walk away with a package in their hands, but if he ran out, he used a subcontractor to drop-ship the product directly to the customer. The subcontractor billed Chuck for the shipping charges and a handling fee. If they didn't ship anything, it didn't cost Chuck anything. Chuck's business was immensely profitable. However, as his organization grew and the volume he was shipping grew, he decided it would be more economical to ship the materials himself. So he secured a warehouse.

But if you have a warehouse, you need a phone and utilities and insurance and someone to run the place. And you have to pay for all of these things every month, whether you ship one item or one thousand items. Not only that, but for Chuck, owning a warehouse was actually contradictory to the underlying emphasis of his original marketing and distribution program. Why? Because Chuck preferred to deliver his product from the back of the seminar room. It was less costly and he never lost the sale. Ideally, he didn't want to have to ship anything at all. By obtaining a warehouse to handle back-table inventory shortages, he was creating a true paradox: stocking, staffing, and paying for a facility he didn't want to use.

What he did was take a revenue cost and convert it into an infrastructure cost. While it's true the warehouse saved him money during periods when he significantly underestimated his sales, it cost him money when his forecasts were on target.

There's an additional problem when you convert a revenue cost into an infrastructure cost, and that is that the infrastructure cost tends to take on a life of its own that is independent of sales.

In Chuck's case, he figured he had this warehouse manager on salary, and he might as well use him as much as possible. That makes sense, but it wasn't long before the warehouse manager was doing so much he needed an assistant. So instead of having a variable cost tied directly to revenue, Chuck had created a fixed cost with no relation to revenue—and it was a fixed cost that kept growing.

Chuck is not the only entrepreneur to make the mistake of taking an extremely adaptable, movable expense and setting it in concrete. When our sporting goods business was in the process of growing from one retail store to nine, we were doing a lot of silk-screening of sports team uniforms, which we subcontracted. We would order the uniforms based on the team's requirements and then take them to the silk-screener, who would print them. He charged us $6.50 for the screen and 60¢ per uniform printed. We charged $9.75 for the screen and 75¢ per uniform printed. So we had an additional revenue source in which we had no capital investment, and it worked great for years.

Then I decided that since we were paying the silk-screener so much for printing each set of uniforms, and he must be making a profit at that price, we should be making that profit ourselves. So I bought a silk-screening machine. But we needed more than the machine; we also needed ink. Not just any old ink, but a latex ink. And we needed the ink in a variety of colors. Not just green and blue and yellow, but in all the school colors. We couldn't have only green; we had to have dark green, forest green, kelly green, light green, and so on. Same thing with all the other colors. But okay, we bought all the ink.

So I had not only the machine, but also all the inks—and we got an order for football uniforms. I prepared the silk screen, I put a jersey on the machine, put the screen on the jersey, and squished the latex ink all over the screen—and all over my hands and face and clothes and shoes. Oh, and one more thing about latex ink: it has to cure. So we spent several thousand dollars on a special oven to use for curing the printed uniforms.

I started as a retailer. I was becoming a printer. I stood to make almost a 50 percent margin on those football jerseys.

I'd printed them—even though I managed to get ink all over myself in the process, I figured I'd get better with practice—and I put them in the oven to cure.

They went in as football jerseys.

They came out as toast.

I had to call a rush order into my uniform supplier and do the whole thing all over again. Obviously, I wasn't making the same profit our silk-screen subcontractor made.

The point is, when I subcontracted the silk-screening process, I kept that expense on a revenue-related basis. I didn't have the cost unless I sold a set of uniforms to a team. But when I brought all that machinery into the store, I turned that revenue-related cost into an infrastructure cost. I had to pay for that equipment whether I used it or not, whether it was making money for me or not.

Another problem with converting revenue expenses to fixed costs is that if the nature of your business should change, you may not be able to modify the fixed cost to your new needs.

Shortly after I decided to do our own silk-screening, our business did in fact change. We began franchising, and instead of team business, we began bidding to institutions for athletic hard goods, such as basketballs, baseballs, and other equipment. And I was stuck with all this equipment, a sea of ink, and an expensive oven that I never did figure out how to use.

This was a major capital investment that did not allow me any maneuverability or adaptability. Had I stayed with the silk-screener, I could have simply gone to him at that point and said, "I really appreciate the business you've done, but we're eliminating the sale of uniforms and apparel from our business. You've done a good job for us over the years, here's a bottle of champagne, and thanks." But I didn't stay with the silk-screener, and even today I remember what that mistake did to the dollars in my pocket.

The most important principle of cost control is to create, as much as you possibly can, a variable relationship between any particular cost and the revenue that's being generated on the cost. Always turn your fixed expenses into variable expenses, not the opposite.

Millie's Millinery did that perfectly in her agreement with Hall's Department Store. Her rent was based on a percentage of her sales. If sales were down, so was the rent. If sales were up, the rent was up, but that was okay because she was making enough money to cover it.

Maintaining a variable relationship between costs and revenue applies not only to supplies and services, but personnel as well. In my law firm, for example, everyone who does work that is billed to clients is paid based on the actual amount of revenue they bill. If the work done by an attorney or a paralegal is billed at $100 per hour, they are paid approximately $25 per hour. They see a direct relationship between what they produce and what they earn.

We don't have salespeople in a law firm, but I have hired them in other businesses, and there is no reason why a salesperson should be on salary. By definition, salespeople earn their way by how much they sell. Give them a draw, but make it based on their performance. That way you always maintain the integrity of the relationship. You know that if you are paying a 10 percent commission on sales and one of your salespeople earns $5,000 one month, you will have $45,000 left over to pay for the cost of the product and contribute to overhead. You'll never begrudge what people who are paid on a variable basis earn, because the more they make, the more your business makes. And it also becomes extremely easy to identify the people who are not functioning in a profitable manner.

There are certain staff functions that must be paid on salary, and these are infrastructure costs you can't do much about. My own secretary is an example. Her time can't be billed out, but what she does is essential to the firm.

But if you have someone on salary, be certain you truly need them. Don't hire a full-time person to do a job that requires just three hours a day and then figure out ways to fill up the rest of that person's time. If the task is not a full-time job—and even if it is—first look for a subcontractor to do the task. For example, depending on the level of your understanding of accounting procedures and the size of your business, you may choose to keep your records yourself. That's certainly okay, but it's been my experience that most entrepreneurs don't want to be bothered with such details. Consider hiring a bookkeeping service that will charge based on the volume of work they do.

For payroll, investigate one of the many companies that will maintain your payroll and all worker-related taxes, and even provide you with a vehicle to offer your employees a better benefits package than you might otherwise be able to. Remember, a lot of entrepreneurs—and you may be one of them—are finding their niche by offering specific business services to other companies that want to downsize.

Take a look at all your fixed expenses with the idea of converting them to variable ones if possible. Some people find fixed expenses provide them with a certain level of comfort. It's the idea that at least they know how much money they're going to have to spend every month. But isn't it truly more comfortable knowing you will spend a percentage of your total revenue, and that if that revenue drops, so will your expenses; if your revenue rises, profits will increase accordingly?

Applying the Tests of Essentiality and Efficiency. After zero-based budgeting and converting fixed into variable expenses, the third cost containment technique is applying the tests of essentiality and efficiency. This answers the question of whether a given expense is absolutely justified. An expense is justified if it is essential to support or expand—not your business, that's too vague—but the marketing, fulfillment, or production legs of your business. The issue here is not how much it will cost, but whether you should spend the money at all.

Certainly the silk-screening equipment I bought would not have passed the test of essentiality. Neither would the way I outfitted Crepes-To-Go. I wanted to decorate each outlet with a particular type of Italian tile. Of course, I could get a better price buying in volume, and I knew I would be expanding this operation. So instead of buying tile for one restaurant, or even two, I bought enough for seven. I built three restaurants before the chain was closed, and I wound up with all that costly leftover imported ceramic tile I couldn't use, taking up space in my warehouse.

When I advised Karl not to move his advertising agency to larger, more expensive offices, I was applying the test of essentiality and efficiency. We looked objectively at the situation and could see no real reason for spending the additional money.

What is the test of essentiality? It's asking yourself, before you buy, if the expenditure in question is absolutely essential to support or expand the marketing, fulfillment, or production of your product or service.

Do you really need whatever it is you're thinking about buying? Will a cellular phone increase your personal productivity enough to justify its cost? Is a laptop computer with more bells and whistles than a cruise ship truly necessary? What about a copy machine that costs more than your parents' first house?

For some purchases, the essentiality test is fairly simple. Do you need your own facsimile machine? Not if you've been averaging one fax transmission a month. But if your weekly fax charges at your neighborhood office supply store are $20 and you or someone on your staff spends three hours running back and forth, you can easily justify buying your own machine for around $400.

If you can't produce figures to support the purchase, but you are convinced it's a good move, find a company that will provide the product or service temporarily as a subcontractor. That will give you an opportunity to evaluate its essentiality. Or consider short-term leases with purchase options. But until you can prove the need for an expense, don't make the purchase.

The flip side of essentiality is efficiency. The decisions that deal with efficiency are often related to how far in the future you are planning. For example, let's say you know you need a computer, and you can get a complete system that will meet your needs today for about $7,000. But you also know you'll outgrow the system within three years. To buy a system that will meet your projected needs for the next five years will cost $10,000. So the question is, do you buy for today at $7,000, or do you spend an additional $3,000 now and buy for three years from today?

My suggestion is to take an intermediate approach to costs, usually twelve to eighteen months. Why? Because there are very few businesses that maintain a consistent course over a period of time. They'll go in one direction for a while, then they'll shift and go in another direction as the market dictates, until ultimately what originally happened in the business is no longer relevant. Businesses find themselves not needing or unable to use equipment they purchased in the past.

Do you need to do long-range planning for your business? Most assuredly. But do you need to do long-range purchasing? Definitely not. I've made those mistakes, and I know they don't make sense. So when you apply the test of efficiency, you don't need to look beyond the next twelve to eighteen months. When you start looking three or five or seven years into the future, you're only guessing.

Spend money if—and only if—there is a valid reason. The only valid reason is when the expense is required to support or expand the marketing, fulfillment services, or production legs of your business. Then apply zero-based budgeting and, if possible, tie the expense to revenue.

Remember, the most efficient cost is not always the cheapest. Determine the quality you need, and then negotiate for the lowest price based on your objectives.

Apply the test of essentiality and efficiency to every purchase, regardless of the amount. It will highlight expenses that are not necessary to your operation, giving you the option to eliminate those costs and increase profitability.

Revenue Enhancement

Profitability comes from two things: reducing costs and increasing revenue. We've talked about cost containment, now let's talk about revenue enhancement.

Revenue enhancement entails pricing for profitability and creating add-on revenue sources. The key is to always price for your market, not from your cost. Here's the formula:

Unit cost + operational (or infrastructure) cost + value = price.

The tendency of most people is to take a look at the unit cost and factor it in some way. Retailers, for example, tend to mark up most items the same percentage, often 100 percent, or a 50 percent gross profit margin. So if a retailer pays $5 for a shirt, he or she will sell it for $10. If a retailer pays $2 for a pair of socks, he or she will sell them for $4.

That's foolish, because in reality, the price you charge doesn't have a whole lot to do with the cost of the unit to you. If it did, that would mean that the more efficient you were at reducing your cost, the less profit you would make.

If I have a 50 percent gross margin on T-shirts in my store, and I've been buying shirts for $5, that means I'm selling them for $10 and making $5 per shirt. But if I find a new supplier and can now get that same shirt for $2, does that mean I ought to reduce the price of the shirt to $4 and bring my gross profit down to $2 per unit? Certainly not.

When you create your pricing structure, focus not on the cost of the item, but on its value. It is value that will ultimately determine the price of a product. But value doesn't just happen; it gets created. There are four different ways you can create value.

Absolute Value. Very few of us create absolute value, and though it's difficult to define, you know it when you see it. Absolute value transcends the dynamics of the marketplace. There's a physician in Orlando who specializes in microsurgery and has had phenomenal success with reattaching severed limbs. If your hand is cut off in an accident and you, along with your severed hand, get to this doctor within a few hours, he can sew your hand back on. After a few months of therapy, your hand will function normally.

How much is that worth?

How much do you have? You're not going to quibble about the surgeon's fee.

That's absolute value, and most products don't have it. If you need brain surgery, you don't shop around for the best price. If you need eyeglasses, you probably will. The point is, if your product or service is virtually priceless, then it has absolute value.

Relative Value. This is the most common way of creating value, and it can come from two directions. The first is when you can show a substantial cost savings from your product or service; the second is when what you're selling will produce more revenue for your customer without costing them significantly more money than they are currently spending.

The value is always relative for your customer, not relative to your cost. Lori Meade's company, Main Events, provided relative value. Her skills in booking hotels and other event coordination tasks saved her clients a substantial amount of money over what it cost them to do it themselves. It's not important to them that it might have taken Lori only an hour to accomplish more than their staff could in an entire day; they paid her for what—and who—she knew and the cost savings they gained from that.

As an attorney, my product is frequently advice, and my cost of delivery might be the price of an hour-long telephone call. The value to my client comes not from the sixty minutes we spend on the phone, but from the interaction that may save my client a lawsuit or otherwise allow him or her to measure the benefit in actual dollars.

That's why many consultants work for a percentage of what they save you with their services. If they save you a lot, they make a lot—regardless of how much time or effort it took for them to do it. If they can't save you anything, it doesn't cost you anything.

Relative value also occurs when your product or service will produce more revenue for your customer. Incomm International is a trade show sales training and research center. The firm's clients know that having their booth staff properly trained will result in increased sales from trade shows. Those increased sales are the relative value of the sales seminar. It doesn't matter what the actual cost of providing the training was to Incomm—the training is worth the relative value.

So when your pricing mechanism reflects the fact that your product value has produced either a higher benefit or a substantial cost savings, you have relative value.

Perceived Benefit. Some advertising and marketing experts would argue that every benefit—including those seen as absolute and relative value—are nothing more than perceived benefits. That might be, but at least for teaching purposes, absolute and relative value appear to be different from perceived benefit.

With this type of value, you're not selling a real benefit in economic terms, you're selling the perception of a benefit. Johnny Walker Black Label is more expensive than Johnny Walker Red Label, but the production costs for the Black Label are not in proportion to the higher retail cost. The value is in perception.

A charity fund-raising ball held at one of Orlando's finest hotels every year costs $150 per couple, and hundreds of people attend. Last year, a different annual ball for another charity was held at the same hotel and featured a similar menu. But tickets for that ball were $600 per couple. The reason? The second ball had a reputation for attracting the cream of society, the local movers and shakers—a perceived benefit.

Even among law firms, there's a perceived benefit in having certain firms represent you. But the real benefit rests with the skill of the particular attorney who is handling your case.

BMW uses the slogan "The ultimate driving machine." Do you know what that means? I don't, but I do know they price their cars accordingly.

There was a time when the public perception of Cadillac was that anybody who was anybody drove one. Fords and Chevrolets could get you where you wanted to go, but if you went in a Cadillac, you went in style. And you believed, based on the perceived benefit, that the price was justified. Now the market position of Cadillac has been eroded by other luxury automobiles, but even in the case of BMW, Volvo, and Mercedes, it is the perceived benefit, not the actual economic benefit, that creates value.

Uniqueness of Source. This method of producing value is nothing more than a legalized monopoly. When you are the only source, and your product is sufficiently different from anything else available in your market niche, you can price according to uniqueness. This ties into eliminating the competition by defining your market niche so narrowly that you have no competition.

Sharper Image is a unique source for electronic playthings. Neiman Marcus carries items you won't find in any other department store.

For small companies, handmade or craft items often provide a uniqueness of source. When Miriam started her calligraphy business and targeted the bridal departments of fine department stores, she had no competition. No one else did what she was doing. The cost of her product was literally pennies for the ink and special pens, but she could charge just about whatever she wanted because she was a unique source. That's how she turned a hobby into a business that provides her with a six-figure income.

A market niche creates a uniqueness of source and produces market dominance and higher profitability. The more narrow your market niche, the more unique you are as a source.

So remember, it's unit cost + operational cost + value = price. There is no pricing maximum when you're dealing with the creation of value. When you add value to a product with absolute or relative value, perceived benefit, or uniqueness of source, you're creating an ability to price at a level that pays both your revenue-related and infrastructure-related costs and leaves you a healthy profit left over.

Understand that this is not the old cliché of pricing according to what the market will bear. The market will only bear the value that's indicated. When Cadillac lost its general perception as being the premium quality automobile, General Motors' margin on the Cadillac division began to erode. BMW's margin didn't erode, nor did

Mercedes's. The market was still willing to pay the price, but people wanted the value.

And you create the value that provides your ultimate profit.

Add-On Revenue Sources

Contain your costs, and price according to value, not cost. Then enhance your income even further through add-on revenue sources.

Add-on revenue sources are things you can do within your existing structure that have little or no impact on your expenses but can produce a significant amount of additional revenue. Begin by identifying the product or service that is your primary revenue center. You then develop add-on revenue sources. Remember Susan, the massage therapist? Her primary revenue center was massages; she created add-on revenue sources with vitamins, lotions, and relaxation tapes.

I was involved in an Italian restaurant, and of course our primary revenue center was our food. We served particularly good pasta, which was especially popular. So we began packaging the pasta and selling it at the front counter. Customers also enjoyed our specialty desserts, which were baked on the premises. So we added a baked goods counter up front. Our soups were delicious. So we arranged to wholesale quantities of soup to other area restaurants. These are all examples of add-on revenue sources.

Finding add-on revenue sources is nothing more than judicious horizontal and vertical expansion, and we'll talk more about this in Chapter Thirteen. The benefit is that you increase your revenue without significantly increasing your costs. The expense involved in selling pasta and desserts to our customers to take home was nominal. Most of the money we made from those sales went straight to the bottom line in the form of additional profit. Once your operation is developed to the point that your primary revenue center is profitable, you augment those profits by tapping into everything you can think of in terms of add-on revenue sources.

Functioning for Cash Management

There are two sides to the financial end of your business. We've already discussed the first, profitability—a necessary component to a successful business. The second is cash management, because you aren't likely to be successful or profitable if you can't manage your cash.

There's more to cash management than simply recording what comes in and what goes out. Of course, cash management is closely tied to profitability, and the principles we have already discussed will aid you in managing your cash. But we need to go further.

You have two primary objectives with cash management: you want to turn all your current assets into cash as rapidly as possible, and you want to minimize or possibly eliminate your fixed asset buildup.

To achieve these goals, you need to be examining your financial reports regularly, especially your asset and liability statement, which we discussed in Chapter Eleven.

Turn Cash Equivalents into Cash

The essence of effective cash management is to convert your cash equivalents back into cash as fast as you can, because the faster you do this, the more profit you make and the more access to cash you have.

Let's compare two stores, both with an inventory of $20,000. The first store has an annual sales volume of $20,000, or we can say it converts its inventory into cash once a year. Assuming a gross profit margin of 50 percent, that's a $10,000 contribution to overhead. The second store, by contrast, has the same inventory and gross profit margin, but it converts that inventory into cash six times a year, or every two months. In that store, there is $120,000 in annual sales, which leaves us with a $60,000 contribution to overhead.

Not only is the second store going to be more profitable, but it will give you more access to cash. Since the inventory is turning six times a year, the store has the cash not only to pay for the inventory, but to contribute to overhead and, ultimately, to profit.

When I was involved in purchasing for my sporting goods store, I made a deal with Spalding at one point and bought ten thousand inflatable balls at an incredibly low price—anywhere from 25 to 35 percent cheaper than the price that any other retailer was able to buy these same goods at. Certainly every time I sold one of those balls, it was extremely profitable.

My problem was that it took me two-and-a-half years to sell them all. And during that period, the balls were tying up space in my ware-house and, more importantly, tying up my cash in inventory. Fortunately, other items were selling well, but for a while we were struggling to pay the bills, thanks to that "great" deal.

If I buy something for three dollars and sell it for twenty, that's a profitable sale. But if it takes me a year to make the sale, who's going to pay the rent in the meantime?

Apply the same principles to your receivables. It doesn't do you any good to have lots of people owing you money if they don't pay you, or if they pay you slowly. You can't pay bills with money someone owes you. That's how the savings and loan associations got in such a mess.

Turn your receivables back into cash as fast as you can. That allows you to buy more inventory, turn the inventory into a receivable, and turn the receivable back into cash. The flow of cash equivalents is the following: cash, inventory, receivables, cash. If you do not extend credit, then the flow is as follows: cash, inventory, cash. The faster and more often you complete that cycle, the more money you'll make and the more liquid you'll be.

If your annual sales and annual receivables are the same, then you are only turning your receivables once a year. That means you have to wait twelve months to get your money back from sales. If your annual sales and receivables were $400,000 and you added on a financing cost of 12 percent, you would be losing $48,000 in interest on the cost of capital for that $400,000 in sales. The solution is not to try to make up for this loss by tacking a finance or service charge onto your receivables; you're not in the lending business. You don't want to collect interest, you want to collect the amount that's owed you so you can buy more inventory and make more money.

You do that by establishing credit policies appropriate to your business and your clientele, and by being prepared to enforce them with sound collection procedures.

Begin by clearly formulating your payment policy. Is it going to be net ten, net thirty, or net forty-five days? In my law firm, it's net ten days. At The Open University, it's C.I.A. (Cash In Advance). In my sporting goods business, it's net thirty days. The other players in your field can provide you with input as to what's most appropriate for your industry.

If certain customers can't meet your payment policy, it might be best not to deal with them. In my sporting goods business, we are a major supplier to agencies in the state of Florida, and they pay in thirty days. But a long time ago I decided not to deal with the federal government because they take too long to pay.

Once your payment policy is set, decide what will be considered past due. Most companies allow a grace period between the time the invoice is actually due and the time it becomes past due. In my law firm, it's twenty days. For my sporting goods business, it's sixty days. Again, let the nature of your business be your guide.

Finally, determine what you will do when an account becomes past due, and do it consistently. Your first step may be just to mark the next statement "past due" in bold red letters. Or you might want to send a letter or give the customer a call.

Your first collection contact should be very gentle. Don't offend anyone; just remind them they owe you money and that you would like for them to pay it. A typical protocol that works well is to say, "Our records indicate we haven't received a payment on your account in thirty days. Can you check your records to see if they agree?" If that doesn't work, your collection efforts can become stronger as needed, up to and including filing suit for the amount due.

You're not doing your customers a favor by allowing them to get past due. In actuality, studies have shown that you're worse off if you don't keep your receivables current. Some customers will be embarrassed by the fact that they haven't paid you and will end up finding another supplier. That leaves you not only with a receivable that's not paid, but a lost customer as well.

By keeping in touch with your customers, you'll know if they are having problems that will affect your future relationship. If they are experiencing temporary cash flow difficulties, you may decide to make special payment arrangements, such as allowing them to pay a portion of the past due amount each month while they stay current on future purchases. Remember, too, that any communication with a customer can—and should—be turned into a sales opportunity, to increase your revenue. You can build tremendous loyalty by being willing to work with a customer.

Minimize Fixed Assets

For the same reason that you want to turn your inventory and receivables into cash as quickly as possible, you also want to minimize your fixed assets and eliminate any nonessential assets. The only value your fixed assets have is the extent to which they allow you to convert a cash equivalent into cash.

I'm sure you've eaten in restaurants where they bring around a dessert cart after dinner. The cart is a fixed asset; the desserts are a cash equivalent. The cart allows the restaurant to display the desserts attractively so they can be sold. Savvy restaurateurs don't invest any more in the cart than they absolutely have to; it doesn't have any real value to them because it can't be converted into cash.

Let's go back to our two-store comparison, but this time, let's say they have equal inventory and equal sales of $50,000 annually. But the first store requires $100,000 of fixed assets to make those sales, and the second requires no fixed assets. If those two stores were for sale, a business broker would value the first business significantly higher than the second because of the fixed assets. But why would you want to pay so much more for a business that earns the same amount of money as one without all those fixed assets to deal with?

When I assist clients in evaluating a business, the only thing that's relevant to me is the business's cash and cash equivalents and how much profit it generates. I don't care how much is invested in fixed assets. If assets don't contribute to a higher profit level, they have no value.

The size of the company doesn't matter. When I was in law school, I used to analyze major companies to determine how much I would pay for them if they were for sale. (I did this just for a hobby; I had no money.) Most of the time, I found that companies had far more in fixed assets than they really needed.

So minimize your fixed assets and get rid of any nonessential assets. A streamlined, efficient operation will have most of its money tied up in the one area that will make it more money: cash or cash equivalents.

Profitability and cash management go hand in hand. Without both, you can't have a successful business. Function for profitability with zero-based budgeting, converting as much of your infrastructure costs to revenue-related costs as possible, and applying the tests of essentiality and efficiency. Then price for profitability by creating value for your product or service, and always be on the lookout for add-on revenue sources. Manage your money by turning your current assets into cash as fast and frequently as possible, while you eliminate or at least minimize your fixed assets.

Functioning for Human Resource Development

Have you noticed that a lot of companies don't have personnel departments anymore? They have *human resources departments,* because they have realized that people are one of their most important components. They are functioning for human resource development.

It's important to understand the economic and demographic forces that are shaping businesses today: the labor force is shrinking and aging, the cost of hiring is increasing, turnover is increasing, and companies are automating and using technology to make fewer workers more productive.

What does this mean to businesses in the nineties? It means coping with a serious shortage of qualified entry-level workers. It means paying the price for top talent. It means absorbing the cost of turnover while always being on the lookout for ways to reduce it. And it means turning to automation and technology whenever possible, for increased productivity.

On the surface, large corporations have an edge over small businesses in attracting the best employees. They have the resources to offer more benefits and, at least up until the past decade, have had the illusion of offering greater stability. But today's worker isn't necessarily looking for stability; in fact, the average graduating college senior will make more than ten job changes in his or her career.

Studies have shown that recognition, appreciation, opportunity for advancement, and a sense of being a valued member of the team are as important to people as salary. We can no longer treat employees like a raw material we buy for production purposes. Even the smallest of companies needs to treat their human resources as the most valuable asset they have.

Develop Competitive Compensation

The first step in doing that is developing competitive compensation, promotion, and incentive policies. You may think you can't afford to pay the same salary as a major corporation and so you can't compete for the best people, but with a little creativity, you can make your company an extremely attractive place to work.

Under the heading Functioning for Profitability, we discussed turning fixed expenses into variable ones. Salaries are a fixed expense; compensation based on performance is a variable one. And by offering a performance-related system, you won't put a cap on any worker's production.

Variable compensation can be based on three things: a percentage of net revenue, a percentage of net profit, or a commission on each unit sold. You can use just one method, or combine them for maximum flexibility. You might also consider offering a base salary with bonuses tied to productivity.

The manager of our sporting goods warehouse receives a percentage of the net profit of the business. If he controls expenses, the business makes more profit, and Steve earns more money. You'll find that top salespeople prefer being paid on commission—they know they can make more money that way. Whenever you can, tie compensation to your business's actual revenue source. You'll make more money, and your "human resources" will be happier.

There still will be some people you must pay on salary, and my advice is to make that salary a little bit higher than the going rate in your community. If you hire the right people, your investment will pay off. For instance, I pay my secretary about 25 percent more than the average legal secretary earns in Orlando. I also travel quite a bit, and when I'm out of town, she has a certain amount of free time. That's okay, because our deal is that when I'm in town, she has to keep up with me. And if I spend the better part of a day dictating, she has those tapes transcribed before the end of the next day, no matter how late she has to stay to do it. So pay more, but demand more. You'll get it.

Remember, compensation is more than just dollars. You need to consider working hours, a vacation plan, paid sick time, holidays, and the like. You also want to offer other fringe benefits, such as employee discounts if your product lends itself to that, or group discounts in local stores or restaurants.

Almost all the major tourist attractions around the country offer discount clubs to employers, and you don't have to be a local company to qualify. Car rental companies offer the same type of deal. One of the easiest ways to provide such benefits is to contract with an organization whose business it is to provide benefit packages for small businesses. Check with the Chamber of Commerce, Better Business Bureau, and other people in your own small business network for referrals.

Another major portion of compensation is insurance. The cost of medical insurance is skyrocketing, and even large companies are now asking workers to contribute to the cost of this benefit. As I write, American businesspeople are waiting to see what action the Clinton administration will take on health care. Whatever that action happens to be, my advice is to shop around for coverage, and allow your staff members to participate in the decision-making process. Offer them choices: would they prefer to pay part of the premium for a lower deductible or have a higher deductible and you pay the entire cost; would they prefer traditional insurance or an HMO plan; do they need options like dental and eye care; are maternity benefits important?

There's more to insurance than just medical. A company-paid life policy—even for a modest amount—says you care about employees' families. Provide short- and long-term disability options. Offer a savings plan through payroll deduction, or a retirement program that will provide tax benefits.

The cost of providing most of these benefits, except for the medical insurance, is nominal, but the return on your investment in terms of production and employee loyalty makes it a wise investment.

Even though you will tie pay to productivity as much as possible, you still need incentive programs. Publicly recognize outstanding performance. Offer cash compensation for cost-saving suggestions. Reward longevity with bonuses and increased benefits. Create a profit-sharing plan to give workers a sense of ownership in the company. Look for ways to express your appreciation, as I did when I took my entire staff to Jamaica to let them know their efforts were not going unnoticed.

Internal Policies

Your employees should feel they have a future with the company. Establish a promote-from-within policy and give everyone a shot at each job opening. Some progressions are obvious: the shipping clerk should be considered for the warehouse manager's job. Others are not so readily apparent: a customer service representative may be the ideal candidate for that open sales territory.

To make this system work, take the time to write detailed job descriptions and requirements—but make sure the requirements are truly necessary. For the sales job, do you really need someone with five years of outside sales experience, or would an enthusiastic self-starter who already knows the company and the customers be more valuable?

Training

Training is another important aspect of human resource development. No matter how skilled a new employee is, he or she will require some training to get up to speed in your organization. And don't overlook the value of ongoing training. A small advertising agency in Orlando hires a temporary receptionist to answer the phones for a half day each month while the entire staff holes up in a conference room at a local hotel for a catered lunch and training. Topics range from technical subjects to personal development, and the payoff is loyal employees who provide clients with a high level of service.

Training comes back to you in a variety of ways. It builds individual self-esteem and employee loyalty. It reduces turnover. It enhances both individual and group skills and maximizes productivity of existing workers. It is truly an investment in the future of your company.

In all of my companies, I encourage my staffers to request training. When they learn of a course being offered that will enhance their skills and increase their value to the company, I am more than willing to pay for it. Consequently, I have a top-notch staff and an extremely low turnover rate. My employees are paid based on what they produce, and they are allowed to grow within the company as much as they want to.

Communication

Finally, have procedures in place for employee review and communication. Everyone needs verbal feedback, even when their paychecks tell them they're doing a good job. They need to know about the big picture—how the company is doing, what the short-term plans and long-range goals are, and how each employee fits into the overall program. And communication is a two-way street. Workers need a vehicle to let you know their feelings and concerns. When they believe the company cares about them, they will care in return.

I make a big deal out of employee reviews. I set aside at least two hours and devote that time exclusively to the person being reviewed— no interruptions of any kind. We go out of the office for breakfast or lunch. I critique their performance, offer suggestions for ways they can enhance their skills in the coming year, and let them know how I will support them in their endeavors. This is also a time for them to be totally candid with me: they give me their assessment of the company, of their coworkers, and of me. Our conversation is totally private, and they know they can say anything they want without fear of recrimination.

The way I handle employee reviews is actually a defensive posture. I never want to be surprised by someone quitting unexpectedly because their position wasn't meeting their needs. I never want to be so out of touch with my employees that I don't know what their objectives and goals are. And I can accomplish that with regular and real communication, both in the formal review process and in the everyday operation of the business.

We haven't come anywhere close to covering all of the nuts and bolts involved in the day-to-day running of a business, but if you will use this system of functional processing—that is, functioning for profitability, cash management, and human resources—to enhance your operational structure, you'll see your business performance improve markedly.

Chapter Twelve Highlights

—Functional processing includes functioning for profitability, cash management, and human resource development.

—Functioning for profitability begins with cost containment. The issues involved include zero-based budgeting, converting fixed expenses into variable expenses, and applying the tests of essentiality and efficiency.

—You can increase revenue by pricing for profitability.

—Create value in your pricing structure with absolute value, relative value, perceived benefit, and uniqueness of source.

—The formula for pricing is unit cost + operational cost + value = price.

—Add-on revenue sources increase profitability without significantly affecting the cost of overhead.

—Effective cash management means turning all your current assets into cash as rapidly as possible and minimizing or eliminating fixed asset buildup.

—Human resources will become increasingly valuable in the 1990s. Function for human resource development with competitive compensation packages, recognition, opportunity, training, and communication.

CHAPTER THIRTEEN

Critical Elements of Profitability
Making Any Business Profitable

"I've been rich and I've been poor. Rich is better."

—Sophie Tucker, Singer

IN CHAPTER TWELVE, you learned about functioning for profitability. Profitability is the natural result of a business operated well. It is also the specific result of the techniques you learned in the last chapter. There are certain critical elements of profitability that, once understood and applied, will help you maximize the profit-making potential of your company.

When I started looking at businesses that were most profitable, it was with the goal of identifying exactly what was making them so profitable. I analyzed over twelve hundred companies before I came up with six critical elements of profitability. These elements can be overlaid onto any business, whether it's a start-up operation, an existing business you own, or one you are considering buying or investing in.

(1) Insensitivity of Price. With insensitivity of price, there is no restriction on what you can sell your goods or services for. You create insensitivity of price every time you create absolute value. You can also create insensitivity of price when you create relative value, a perceived benefit, or uniqueness of source.

When I was in college, I came home on a break, as I usually did, to work in the family sporting goods store. I noticed a full-page ad by a major discount department store in the local paper that announced, among other things, that a Zebco rod and reel was available for $9.95. We carried that same rod and reel, but it cost us $12 and we sold it for $21.95. Or, rather, we priced it at $21.95; we didn't sell too many of them. Why should anyone pay us $21.95 for a product they could get elsewhere for less than half that? There was no particular benefit in buying from us rather than the discount store. It was the exact same rod and reel, so there was no absolute or relative value, nor was there a uniqueness of source.

A fundamental rule of business is to buy low and sell high. When you reverse that process, you don't make much money. In the case of the rod and reel, and a lot of other items, we didn't have insensitivity of price. Quite the contrary—at that time we were very sensitive to price. We had extremely narrow margins on a lot of items, and we lost money on some things to remain competitive in the marketplace. We had to make some major changes in the lines we carried and the markets we targeted to develop an insensitivity to price.

When you have insensitivity of price, you have a whole different story from the one we had with our fishing gear. There's a law firm in Miami that specializes in representing Latin American companies that want to buy United States banks. The law firm finds the banks and puts the deal together, and their fee is a flat $100,000. How much does it cost them to provide this service? Two paralegals and two lawyers spend about three weeks working on the documentation. In real dollars, that translates to about $9,000. So they spend $9,000 to earn a $100,000 fee.

Is that insensitivity of price? Most certainly. Because they have uniqueness of source, which is another critical element of profitability. How many law firms specialize in representing Latin American companies that want to buy U. S. banks? I'm not sure, but I suspect very few. Only one—the one in Miami—comes readily to mind. So they can name their price.

Remember, your ability to create value—the very same things that produced value in the last chapter—will also allow you to create insensitivity of price.

(2) Fungibility of Costs. This element of profitability goes hand in hand with insensitivity of price, except that it focuses on the production cost rather than the sale price. Fungible is a term which, when used

in this sense, means that the cost of what I am selling is immaterial in relationship to how I price it. When you have fungibility of costs, you will have increased profitability.

In my sporting goods business, we didn't have fungible costs, we had hard costs. A basketball cost me $10, I sold it for $17.95. A pair of running shoes cost me $25, I sold them for $45 or less. These are not fungible costs; they are hard costs.

By contrast, when you stop at a kiosk in a shopping mall for a cup of espresso and a chocolate eclair, you're buying items that have fungible costs. You pay $1.50 for the cup of espresso and $4 for the eclair. But the espresso costs about seven cents to make, and the eclair costs the restaurant owner a whopping 40¢. These are fungible costs, because their relationship to the sales price of the item is almost irrelevant.

Such costs are readily apparent when you look at your profit and loss statement, because they are nominal when compared to gross revenue. In Chapter Eleven, we talked about the average breakdown of income and expenses for businesses today and said that the cost of revenue was 65 percent of the gross revenue. With fungible costs, your cost of revenue can easily drop to 25, or 15, or even 10 percent of the gross revenue. If your infrastructure costs remain at 29½ percent, that means your net profit could range from 45 to 60 percent—a marked improvement over the 5½ percent national average.

Remember our sample profit and loss statement? Without fungible costs, Complete Industrial Products showed a net profit of $825 for the month. But what if the company had fungible costs and the cost of inventory was only $1,500 instead of $6,500? That would drop their total cost of revenue from $9,750 to $4,750—32 percent of the total revenue—and raise their net profit to $5,825, or 39 percent of the total revenue.

Fungibility of costs is precisely why the information industry is so profitable. The Open University basically runs on fungible costs. Take, for example, *The Desktop Lawyer,* which costs me about $52 in paper, printing, binding, cassette tapes, disks, and packaging. It has sold for as much at $595. Why? Because the actual cost of the book and tapes is immaterial; the value comes from the information they contain. A major publisher puts out a daily newsletter tracking events in the oil industry worldwide and charges over $4,000 for a one-year subscription. It costs less than $300 per year per subscriber to produce and distribute the newsletter, but that doesn't matter to the subscribers. The value is in the information, not in the cost.

When the cost of your product has only an insignificant relationship to the price you can sell it for, you have fungibility of costs—and much healthier profitability.

(3) Add-On Revenue Sources. If you have a one-product, one-distribution system company, you are automatically restricting your ability to add substantial profits to your bottom line. I've talked about add-on revenue sources before. Expanding our retail sporting goods operation to include institutional sales, and then to wholesaling to other retail stores, was an identification of add-on revenue sources. Selling freshly made pasta and desserts at the front counter of our Italian restaurant was another identification of add-on revenue sources.

A popular misconception is that expanding a business means replicating it, but that's not entirely true. Certainly, if you have a successful operation, you can expand that operation by opening another location. When you do that, you may increase your revenue, however you also increase your overhead. I expanded my sporting goods business to nine retail stores before I realized how stupid that was. It's much more efficient and profitable to maintain the same overhead structure and expand your income through add-on revenue sources. Let your income increase while your infrastructure costs remain constant, or at least marginally constant.

Don't replicate your business until you have exhausted every possible opportunity for creating add-on revenue sources.

(4) Minimizing of Operational Costs. When we discussed financial structure, we said you have only two sources of costs: revenue and operations. If you apply the second critical element of profitability and make your revenue costs fungible, your natural corresponding action is to do whatever you can to reduce your operating costs.

One of the basic problems of American businesses is they are spending far too much money on operations and creating infrastructures that are far too expensive in relation to the sales being generated. Be consistent in your application of the tests of essentiality and efficiency. If you don't need it and it won't add to your bottom-line profits, don't buy it.

It is through minimizing of operational costs that small businesses will take on the giants—and win. I maintain that the future of this country lies with its cottage industries—small businesses with minimal infrastructures being run very successfully from spare bedrooms or garages.

If you have a business that operates with an outlay of $20,000 per year and makes $100,000, and your neighbor has a business that generates $500,000 a year but requires $420,000 to operate, your business is going to be more valuable. The reason is that your business allows you to pull out a larger percentage of your revenue as profit. And profit is, after all, the best reflection of whether your business is operating well.

(5) Availability of Targeted Markets. If you have to market to the whole world, two things happen: you'll spend a tremendous amount of money and you won't be very effective. On the other hand, if your market is very targeted, you can spend more money per contact for significantly better results and invest less overall.

If your market is 20 million people, it's going to cost you a fortune to reach them all. Even with a budget of $2 million, that means you only have 10¢ per contact. And I don't know of any small business with a marketing budget of $2 million. In addition, how effective will you be at selling a prospect if you can only spend 10¢ per contact to do it?

If, by contrast, your market is only five thousand people, the situation is totally different. Now you're not trying to sell to "everybody," but instead you are marketing to, for example, owners of Samoyed puppies. Your market research has told you that there are approximately five thousand such owners in the United States. You can find them easily because most of these puppies are registered. You can spend $1 per contact—ten times more than in the previous situation—making your marketing efforts much more effective, and only spend $5,000 total in the process.

The availability of targeted markets allows you to spend less total money on marketing while communicating much more effectively. By going through integrational processing, you have defined the market you intend to target for your business. Stick to it. Recognize not only the underpinnings of a very successful business, but one far more profitable than the norm.

(6) Finding a Defined Solution to a Critical Function. Every business has a critical function that makes everything else happen. It's the heart and soul of the business.

For retailers, it's foot traffic—getting people in the door. They won't buy until they come in. If you don't hear feet in your store every day, you won't be in business for long. So the critical function in any retail business is how to increase foot traffic, not car traffic. People buy. Cars do not. And the retailer who is truly successful is the one who defines new solutions to the critical function of increasing foot traffic.

In restaurants, it's table turns—how long it takes you to serve a meal, move those patrons along, and seat another party. It doesn't matter if you have a line that stretches around the block of people waiting to get into your restaurant, if they can't sit down and eat, they're not going to pay you any money. If you can't turn your tables more than once a night in the typical restaurant, you'll be out of business in six months. Turn them two times, and you'll manage to stay open. Turn your tables three times, and you'll make a profit; four times, and you'll be doing outstandingly well.

So if you are or want to be in the restaurant business, look for ways to increase the table turns. You might have the waiter suggest that customers have their desserts and after-dinner coffee in the lounge by the fire. While they're charmed by both the atmosphere and the consideration of your server, he's gotten them up from the table, sold them an additional item, and cleared the way for another dinner party. That's a defined solution to a critical function, and there are lots of others.

In the seminar business, the critical function is not teaching. Seminar promoters can find someone with the expertise to teach you just about anything you want to know. The seminar content is not the point. What is important is how to match up that information with people who are willing to pay to sit in a seat and listen. So the critical function in the seminar business is putting people in seats.

What is the critical function in your business, and what is the solution for it? These determinations will allow you to focus your efforts on what will enhance your profitability significantly.

Take a moment to read through these critical elements of profitability again. They are simple, easy to understand and apply, and can turn your business into a powerhouse of profits.

Chapter Thirteen Highlights

—There are six critical elements of profitability that can increase the profits of any business.

—Insensitivity of price means there is no restriction on what you can sell your product for.

—Fungibility of costs means the cost of the item you are selling is immaterial in relationship to how you price it.

—Add-on revenue sources allow you to increase revenue without increasing overhead.

—Minimization of operational costs increases profits by decreasing costs.

—Availability of target markets allows your marketing efforts to be more effective while they cost less.

—Finding a defined solution to a critical function means understanding how to find and define a critical solution to the heart and soul of your business operation.

CHAPTER FOURTEEN

Putting Your Ideas in Motion
Where to Start Monday Morning

"Don't be afraid to take a big step if one is indicated. You can't cross a chasm in two small jumps."
—David Lloyd George, Prime Minister of England, 1916–1922

IS THERE MORE TO STARTING and growing your own business than what we've discussed in this book? Of course there is. These are just the basics, the fundamental principles that will allow you to choose a business that is right for you and make it a profitable venture.

Integrational processing takes you beyond the proliferation of self-help courses on the market today. It was designed as a business tool, but the thought processes it provokes will aid you in your personal life as well. Once you have completed the entire integrational processing exercise, put it in a safe place. Refer to it frequently so you stay on track. And update it once a year as circumstances in your life change.

Remember, too, to build integrity into every aspect of your business. An honest, ethical operation is essential for ongoing success. Sure, you can make money with less than forthright habits, and we all know of outright crooks that have made fortunes. But, as the saying goes—and certainly from my experience—what goes around really does come around. Integrity works. It really does.

Building a Business Plan

What you and I have done with *Finding Your Niche* is gone through a step-by-step process that not only reflects the key ingredients of building a business, but also results ultimately in a business plan for your company. Think about it.

Integrational processing gave you what you needed to choose the right business. The chapters on marketing helped you develop a marketing plan. The information on fulfillment services told you what you needed to know to create an effective distribution and delivery system. What you learned about production became your production plan. The chapter on operations told you how to develop your infrastructure, or what is known as an operational plan. Chapters Twelve and Thirteen taught you how to maximize your profits.

Put that all together, and you have a business plan, a road map for your business. Your business plan doesn't have to be complicated. You just developed one. And it doesn't have to be especially long; six pages is usually ample. But it does need to be very specific about what you intend to do and how you intend to do it.

Where do you start? Use the following checklist as a guide.

1. Establish your personal identification and clarify your personal commitment.
2. Develop your business identification and create a business mission statement.
3. Develop your market identification and market position statement.
4. Make sure your focus is clear.
5. Let the focus build natural momentum.
6. Know and establish your market niche.
7. Refine your niche so carefully that you can target your customers and dominate your market.
8. Sidestep the competition.
9. Streamline your business.
10. Develop a marketing plan around what makes you different.
11. Test constantly.
12. Create one or more distribution systems.
13. Arrange for an appropriate delivery system or systems.

14. Determine your primary value-added and set up an efficient production process.
15. Design an infrastructure that will support your business while keeping expenses to a minimum.
16. Be sensitive to profitability and cash management.
17. Price for profitability.
18. Apply the six critical elements of profitability.

Summarize all of that in no more than six pages, call it your business plan, and refer to it as a guide to your business.

If I were to try to summarize this entire book into three essential questions, they would look like this:

1. Who is your customer?
2. What makes you different?
3. What value does your customer obtain through you?

Frankly, the answers to those questions define the scope of your business. Understand them, and you're ready to rollout.

I'm not going to wish you good luck. You won't need it. You have the information you need to start, succeed, and profit as an entrepreneur in the 1990s.

But I do want to know how you do. Drop me a line. Stop me in an airport. But do let me know.

About the Author

Laurence J. Pino founded The Open University, America's College of Wealth Building, to promote entrepreneurism. The University's individual colleges provide comprehensive courses and expert instruction on entrepreneurial activities.

The Open University offers a wide range of intensive week-long courses, day seminars, and home study programs, as well as a total alumni support package.

For more information and a free six-month subscription to *Wealth Builder Monthly*, contact:

The Open University
P.O. Box 1511
Orlando, FL 32802
(800) 874-0388